Dennis —

Best Wishes And

Good luck learning this

Best of all possible methods

Dan Sharper

YOU CAN KILL IT TOO

When the body is used correctly and the club is swung properly we can produce a lot of power. Think about it, the ball is small and very responsive, the club shaft is long and springy, and the shaft is one of many levers the body uses. Furthermore, we weigh hundreds of times as much as the projectile we are launching. You should be surprised if the ball does not go far. If your current swing is weak and the ball does not travel as far as you would like, you will find the answers to your problems here. The distance you want is within you. Best of all, you do not have to be 6'5" tall and have huge muscles. Along with this increase in distance will come the bonus of an equal increase in accuracy due to more precise mechanics.

Players lacking distance is very common. The average player is not getting anywhere near the energy transfer between himself and the ball that he is capable of getting. Weak shots are the product of poor mechanics, usually caused by getting the body and the club into a position where the player cannot use the body weight or the levers of the spine, arms, legs and hands in a powerful manner. Out of position players, in an attempt to hit the ball farther, add more muscular effort. If the body's weight is not used correctly, swinging harder with the arms and legs will do nothing to increase power. In fact, it will reduce your power and cost you distance.

When the body's weight is used in a way that helps produce power we will find that we can actually reduce the effort we use. Then, because our swing is powered correctly, we can increase our efficiency by getting our arms, legs and hands into the proper leverage position so they can all work together. By hitting powerfully with reduced effort we will also gain accuracy and, thus, save our energy for thinking our way around the golf course.

The increase in power you will get from this book should be significant. But power without control is worthless. The things that you will learn here will not only increase your power but, more importantly, they will also give you solid consistent contact. You will have the club head both centered on the ball and also square and traveling directly down the line of flight. This combination of controlled power and solid contact will produce precision ball striking and predictable ball flight.

All we have to do to hit the ball hard is use the body weight to power the pivot as we maintain a fixed swing-circle-center. This will control the location and position of the levers of the arms and hands that, in turn, will swing and control the club head and club face. The body will swing the arms as the hands swing the club.

The information you need is in this book. The learning is up to you.

How to "Kill" the Ball

THE FORMULA

FOR

POWER

AND

ACCURACY

$$E = \frac{mv^2}{2}$$

By Dan Shauger

With Mike Dunaway and Jaacob Bowden

THE MIKE AUSTIN METHOD

Dedicated to the ladies in my life: My Mom, Marion, Diane and Lora. Also to Mrs. Tanya Austin.

**ISBN # 0-9746114-1-7
PUBLISHED BY TWO DOWN PRESS INC.
PRINTED IN THE USA**

ACKNOWLEDGEMENTS

The book you are about to read came about only because the author received a great deal of help from many wonderful souls and wishes to thank the following people:

Dr. Michael Hoke Austin for the sharing of his knowledge and his guidance in passing on the studies of a lifetime. Without his knowledge this book would never have been conceived.

To my good friend, Orlando De Guevara, for all of his help with the camera, the computer and the programs that made all of this possible. Without his help this book would have been scribbled in pencil on a brown paper bag. And, with my handwriting, it would have taken several Egyptologists decades to decipher.

Many thanks to Jaacob Bowden for posing for the pictures and for proving the soundness of the method. I wish him continued success in his long driving and will assist him in achieving his goal of going all the way to the highest level of success on the PGA tour.

Thanks, also, to Christian Wilde for urging this lazy old golf pro to share this knowledge in print. I sincerely hope his book is a blockbuster and it should be read by anyone who has a heart.

Many thanks to Phil Reed for his advice on style and his knowledge of editing and distribution. His book, *In Search Of The Greatest Swing,* should be read in conjunction with this book. It tells much about the exploits and life of the creator of this wonderful method and his own personal search to find the perfect golf swing. It is a delight to read. I also owe him a thank you for introducing me to the work of William Strunk Jr. & E. B. White.

Thanks, also, to Mike Dunaway for the photos and help with promotion. Mike has worked with Mike Austin on all of his video tapes and has demonstrated "the method" and won long driving contests worldwide. Here's to his continued success, health and happiness.

Finally thanks must go out to Cherie Pardo for the final copy edit that makes all this readable.

FOREWORD BY JAACOB BOWDEN

I first met Dan Shauger on a cold and extremely windy day in January of 2003 on the driving range of Lost Canyons Golf Club in Simi Valley, California.

The winds were gusting so furiously that it was nearly impossible to keep our bags from blowing over, our hats on our heads and our balance. Dan was hitting balls behind me, and as I took a backswing to hit the ball an especially hard gust blew me backwards nearly onto him. I may well have bumped into him, were it not for the same gust of wind blowing him backwards as well.

We chuckled over our dedication to practicing in such adverse conditions and we began talking about our respective backgrounds. Dan was soon to turn 63, was retired from a career in the movie industry, and had been teaching golf in the Los Angeles area for the last seven years. He was at Lost Canyons that day because he was considering membership. I had turned 27 earlier in the month, and had recently resigned from a computer engineering job that I had unhappily held in Kansas City and St. Louis for the last four and one half years. I had packed all of my belongings, left my home, friends and family and moved to California to pursue my dream of being a professional golfer on the PGA tour.

At the time I was a 14 handicap and was rather unspectacular at golf; however, both through my own study and also from two or three lessons from a PGA teaching professional, I had become fairly familiar with the fundamentals that were currently being taught by the golf world. I was set on using my time and my $40,000 in savings from my old job to become good enough to turn pro by the end of the year. It was an outrageous goal, but I was young, adventurous and willing to make whatever sacrifice or risk necessary to achieve my goal.

They say that when the student is ready, the master will appear. In our case, I think it could also be said that when the master is ready the student will appear. I believe that Dan and I met for a reason. We needed one another to help fulfill each others' goals. Dan knew more about the golf swing than anyone I had ever met. He had studied closely under the legendary Mike Austin who had given Dan an understanding of a different way of swinging the golf club. Dan told me of Mike's 515 yard drive hit with the unique swing he developed and how he trained Dan to be a teaching professional. The story intrigued me and I decided

I was looking for an edge, and since I was financially limited, I needed some-one like Dan to take me under his wing. The fundamentals that Dan professed were out of the ordinary, yet at the same time his ideas made sense. He was looking for a young, dedicated protege who would listen and and be open to what he had to say. He needed someone who would pick up on his teachings and then go out and prove that his revolutionary teachings worked by having his student win at the highest levels of golf. That was how the relationship be-gan. Dan and I worked together fairly heavily for four or five days each week in February and March, braving cold days and fierce winds. At first my drives were all over the place and each day I had no idea what was in store for me.

By April I was getting so long and straight that someone suggested entering a long drive contest. I entered my first competition in May 2003 in Phoenix, Az. I took 8th place out of over 120 competitors with a 343 yard drive. In my 5th event I beat out over 150 competitors by hitting one 381 yards to win the Pinnacle Distance Challenge in St. Louis! Over the rest of the 2003 season, I realized my dream of becoming a professional golfer, entered approximately 15-18 long drive championships, averaged 336.8 yards per drive, never once completely missed the grid, got to the District Finals of the Remax World Long Drive Championships, increased my clubhead speed to 144 mph, hit one of my drives 400 yards in a mini tour event with a (44 inch driver), lowered my best 18 hole score from 78 to 69, and eliminated all of the back and knee pain I was having using the fundamentals commonly taught in golf today.

Without Dan's knowledge and support, I never would have come close to accomplishing what I did in 2003. And it is this knowledge and support that I hope will take me to the top of the golf world. There truly is a golf swing that is long, straight and easy on the body. Dan knows how to teach it. Many of the concepts he will introduce to you will seem to be the reverse of what is taught in todays market, but trust them and learn with an open mind. By doing so you will soon have an effortless-looking, beautiful, and powerful golf swing that I use to hit those long and straight, drives that most people only dream about.

Thank you Dan, for everything that you have done for me. You are without a doubt the number one teacher in the game of golf, and what you have to offer will revolutionize the way the game is played.

Jaacob Bowden
Winner of the Pinnacle Distance Challenge, St.Louis Mo. 2003

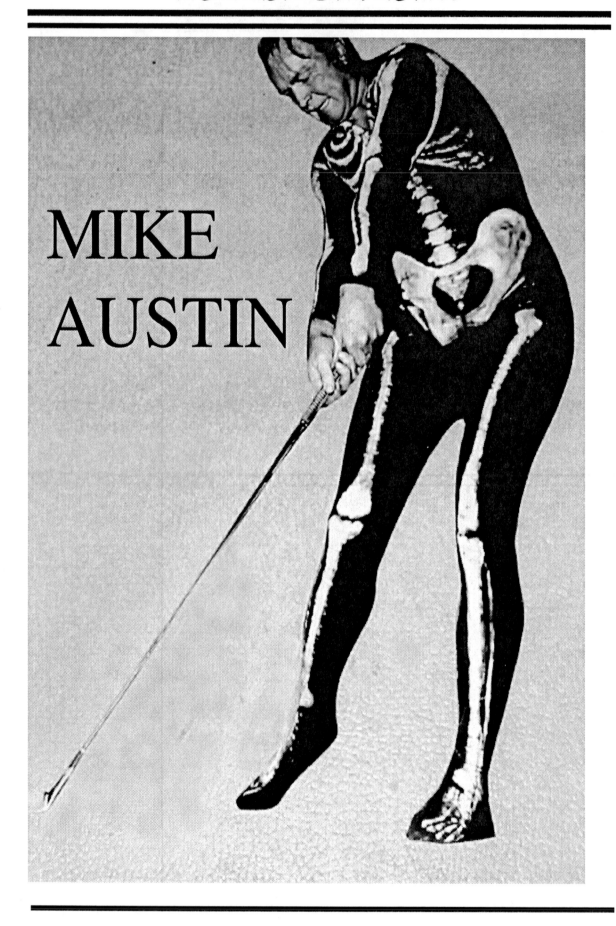

MIKE

AUSTIN

PREFACE

I first met Dan Shauger in 1979 and we have been close friends ever since. We started out as teacher and student but now have developed a friendship that has progressed to a father and son relationship.

Dan has a very sharp and inquisitive mind. When he grasps a concept he is able to take a complex idea and interpret it with simple and easily understood analogies. The words he uses are carefully chosen and describe my method in a very precise manner.

The sketches he has made and the photos with their captions show how well he understands all that I have taught him over the years. He has done a masterful job of interpreting my scientific and medical terms into something the man on the street can easily understand. Dan's background as a construction coordinator in the movie industry has allowed him to hone his mechanical skills to a fine edge. His ability as a golf teacher and golf instructional writer are unparalleled.

After his retirement from the studios, during the years he taught at the Wilson and Harding courses for my dear friends Tom and Roger Barber, he was one of the most sought after teachers in the Los Angeles area. In my opinion, Dan has become the best teacher around because of his ability to see the errors in the golf swing instantly and describe what to do about it. He understands the meaning of every word he uses and does not guess what the result of changing an action will be, he is certain of the outcome.

This book will speak for itself and does not need interpretation. Furthermore, anyone who isn't accredited in the Austin method would not be able to properly interpret it.

No one else could have written this book, it will change the vision of the golf swing from now on.

Michael H Austin Sept. 23, 2003

THE STRUCTURE OF THE BOOK

This book approaches the problem of learning a superior golf swing both as a picture book and as an in depth text book. It's designed this way so the learning will be rapid when used as a visual guide. For study by the serious player the knowledge will be of great depth.

This book will explain the differences between our swing and what I call the common golf swing. This common swing is taught in many fashions all of which are variations of what I call the roller swing. As Mike Austin says, "The same girl in a different dress." In these swings the club face rolls from open to closed as the forearms turn over through the impact area.

- We first will learn a unique way of releasing the club from the wrist joints that will also prove to be an excellent way of chipping the ball. Thus, as we practice our chips we will also be training our wrists in the pattern that they will follow during the full swing release.

- Next we will explain the pivot. If you are already an accomplished player do not make the assumption that you already pivot correctly. The body action we use creates compound leverage and is unique to this type of swing. It must be performed as specified or the entire package will be flawed. It is a major power producer.

- Later we will be learning the combined motions of the hands, arms and shoulders. These are the lever assemblies that are attached to the top end of the spine which control the swinging club head. In this section we will introduce the cranked lever assembly and the concept of the rotating plane.

- Finally, we put the whole swing together. This method of learning is very similar to the way a film is constructed; many scenes are filmed and later edited into the finished product. Hopefully, not too much information will end up on the cutting room floor.

TABLE OF CONTENTS

CHAPTER
1

THE MIKE AUSTIN
METHOD

MIKE AUSTIN, THE MAN AND HIS METHOD

Just in case you are not familiar with Mike Austin's name, I will provide a bit of history. The following is an excerpt from a story titled "The Man Who Cracked the Code" from the pages of The *Los Angeles Times*, October 7, 2001. The piece appeared in the Sunday magazine and was written by Philip Reed.

In the final round of last January's Mercedes Championships, Ernie Ells and Tiger Woods, two of the Tours longest hitters, launched mammoth drives on the downhill, downwind par-5 18th hole of the Plantation Course at Kapalua in Hawaii. Woods' drive stopped 378 yards away. Ells' ball came to rest next to Woods'. Big hits? Yes, but they don't even come close to matching the 515 yard drive of Mike Austin in the 1974 U.S. National Senior Open. That tee shot is listed in the Guinness Book of Records as the longest ever hit in competition. More amazing, Austin was 64 years old when he crushed his record drive. The record still stands

This tee shot was also assisted by a 25 mph tail wind. However, it was on level ground and was hit with a 43 1/2" long driver with a steel shaft and a persimmon head with the old-fashioned wound ball, which was the technology of that era.

There is no telling how far Mike might have been able to hit the new 3-piece solid core rockets we call golf balls. Or, if he could have been assisted by the much longer length and more responsive modern graphite shafts coupled with the springboard-faced titanium club heads currently on the market.

That tee shot was not the only such drive for him. He has won countless long driving contests. He is also renowned for the remarkable record he set while traveling with the 350 Club, (America's long driving team). In many competitions world wide, between the ages of 75 and 79, he averaged an incredible 312 yards.

As of this writing John Daly leads the tour by averaging 309 yards.

At this writing, Mike is still teaching golf despite having had a devastating stroke 13 years ago which left him with a paralyzed right side and having survived a recent fall which fractured his hip and nearly killed him.

Austin's power was only exceeded by his accuracy due to his phenomenal golf swing, which was extremely efficient, perfectly balanced and timed. His swing was a sight to behold. Those fortunate enough to have seen it will tell you it boggled the mind to see the distance he obtained without looking like he was swinging very hard at all. The still photo in the skeleton suit may give you a glimpse of the power of his swing.

Austin formulated the awesome power and accuracy of this swing 50 years ahead of his time by earning degrees in physics, engineering, physiology and psychology. To help explain what he was doing he later received a degree in kinesiology from the National Academy of Applied Science in 1946. Kinesiology is the study of human muscular and skeletal movements, which when properly applied, allows maximum efficiency of the skeleton, combined with the muscles (power producers), and has been a tool used widely in the training of modern track and field athletes with phenomenal results. He pioneered the use of kinesiology in golf and is, without a doubt, unequaled in his understanding of the combined subjects of golf, physics, mechanical engineering and kinesiology.

All of Austin's golf knowledge and his unique ability to integrate those related sciences with his total understanding of the human body made him, in many peoples opinions, the greatest teacher of all time. He has given many thousands of golf lessons to celebrities and other professionals too numerous to mention. In the 1950's he had a television show in Los Angeles about the golf swing and, today, is still widely sought after as a teacher. He was listed as one of Americas top 100 teaching professionals by Golf Magazine until his stroke slowed down his lesson schedule.

Austin is a life member of the PGA and was named Southern California PGA Professional of the year in 1994. He has trained many long drivers of the ball, the most prominent of whom is Mike Dunaway, world champion and author of the book "Hit It Hard," who appears on the cover of this book. Following are some things that have been said about Dunaway: Greg Norman said, "This man is the longest driver in the world." Ken Venturi wrote, "Mike Dunaway combines power and accuracy with a driver better than anyone I have ever seen" and Tommy Aaron remarked, "If Iron Byron ever breaks down they can replace it with Mike Dunaway." I could quote many more just like these.

Your author and guide to this method studied and was guided by this great gentleman for 25 years. However, don't think that it will take you that long to learn it. Quite the contrary. Here, using simple analogies, I will enable you to grasp the concept and the essential movements needed in a short amount of time. Since the actions of the various body parts are easy to perform we will just have to link them together to form the total swing.

Jaacob Bowden, who you will see in the photos in this book, met me in January of 2003 when he was a 14 handicap. After only 4 months of lessons he went from averaging about 250 yards on his drives, and not very straight, to being a scratch player and a winner on the long drive and mini tour circuit.

Less than 5 months after his first lesson and in his first attempt in a long driving contest he finished 8th out of 120 + competitors with a drive of 343 in the grid. He hit several longer than that but they were out, including one that would have won the contest had it not barely missed the grid. He continued to improve over the next few weeks and in his third outing finished fourth. In his fifth outing he won the contest, The Pinnacle Distance Challenge, in St. Louis, Missouri with a drive of 381 yards which must have been most gratifying to him since St. Louis is his hometown. In his next outing, in Oklahoma, he hit the ball 395 on level ground with no wind and again finished fourth. His swing does not look like a drunk at a driving range. It is very smooth and looks very professional.

Anyone who has witnessed a long driving contest knows that most long drivers do not have pretty swings. Jaacob, I am proud to say, is an exception and is proving the method by being very consistent and placing highly in every outing against some very large (6'4" or more and 250+ lb.) and very strong hitters, he is small for a long driver at 6' 2" and 210 lbs.

The editing of the style of this book is the work of a fine writer and editor in his own right, Philip Reed, author of the newspaper article mentioned earlier and the book Free Throw with Dr. Tom Amberry, holder of the world's free throw record of 2,750 consecutive free throws. His latest book, *In Search of the Greatest Golf Swing* is a delight to read and also deals with Austin's knowledge as well as Philip's friendship with him.

This book contains the cumulative knowledge of over 70 years of research by one of the finest minds the world has ever known. He is truly amazing.

I say amazing since his life's accomplishments are nothing short of that, this man who is still actively teaching golf was hitting huge drives in the 1930's. If I were to tell you all that he has accomplished, not only in golf but also many other fields, this book would be just as large but with very little about the golf swing. As Mike Dunaway said, "Compared to Mike Austin, Indiana Jones is a cub scout."

In your authors opinion Michael Austin is the Leonardo Da Vinci of the golf swing. If Da Vinci were alive today, and played golf, this is the swing he would have created.

Austin had the education necessary to invent his own swing by earning degrees in the sciences of physics, mechanical engineering and kinesiology. Using this knowledge he thought up the movements necessary and also developed the verbal skills to pass this knowledge on to others. He has produced several video tapes showing his method and has given seminars worldwide.

Due to the depth of his intelligence and his education he would teach his students in terms that sometimes were beyond the scope of their understanding. He would often be giving a lesson in human muscularity and skeletal medical terms as well as how these things were used in the golf swing.

Your author has made this work free from medical terminology. This book shows Austin's method completely. For the first time it will be described in layman's terms and in a manner enabling the reader to understand the moves and create a sound motion thus improving rapidly. In some instances medical or engineering terms will be used; however, easy to understand drawings and photos will clarify their meaning.

CHAPTER 2

THE EVOLUTION OF THE SWING

IN THE BEGINNING THERE WAS (NOT MUCH) LIGHT

When the first golfers set about trying to learn this most challenging of all games, they were in exactly the same place, knowledge wise, that beginning golfers are today. If you look at the earliest photos of golfers you will see that they look just like modern beginners except for the equipment and the clothing.

This is because the early golfers, just like the modern beginners, simply grabbed the club with both hands and did whatever felt right in order to propel their pellets as far and straight as possible. In other words, the fundamentals of stance, grip and posture either hadn't been stumbled upon, in the case of the first players, or learned from others as is the case of the modern neophyte.

Nearly every modern golf instructor agrees that the grip, stance and posture adapted by almost all top players are the main reasons they strike the ball well. However anyone who digs deeper into the published works and video teachings of the modern top teachers finds a wide range of disagreement as to what the rest of the fundamentals are. Yet, somehow all of the books currently on the market say the same old thing and very little modern information is surfacing.

The golf swing as we know it is the result of the accumulated knowledge of the players who have become proficient at the game. This knowledge has been passed on as correct to each new generation of players. The golf swing, as it is taught today, is still very similar to what players were doing in the 1950's with only detail changes. Film and video technology has allowed the close examination of the swings of the most accomplished players. Using these technologies teachers and players are now better able to refine and gain consistency in the ability to hit the ball.

However, the movements now being taught are not the most scientifically precise and powerful motion that the body is capable of doing. Here, we will examine some of the things we can change to eliminate unnecessary movements as we also improve the movements vital to maximum power, precision ball striking and complete ball flight control.

THE CONCEPT OF THE GOLF SWING

If you were to film a complete novice or a touring pro hitting balls with any one club and overlay each one's replays you would see, as you expect, that the professional would swing the same way every time. Surprisingly so would the novice. Even if his swing looked like he was killing an attacking badger, his move would also have the same look every time. Golfers of every level do this and, in my experience as a teacher, I attribute this to the player's mental concept of the swing. In other words, our bodies make the motions that our minds think need to be done in order to accomplish the swing. So we keep thinking and doing the same things expecting different results. Grooving our move and getting good at being bad. How many of your buddies can you spot two fairways away just from their swing?

I find that changing the way the student mentally sees what he wants to do causes the motion to change instantly. If we get a different idea of how we should go about doing something, the new concept instantly makes the physical changes to our motion. To this end, I will break the golf swing into pieces and show how each piece works in the perfect swing. Then, I will put all the pieces together to show how the swing works when the parts are assembled. All of the pieces as they are described will begin to form our concept of what we are doing. Later, the assembled pieces will blend into a very simple concept that will provide the power and accuracy that we seek. Although we will describe the body's actions separately to facilitate learning, they must ultimately be used as one.

What the mind can conceive the body can do when we obey the laws of physics and use the human machine according to its design. Here, you will find the understanding and the scientific knowledge of how the Austin method works. When the mind grasps the simplicity of the movements the body will produce golf shots that are absolutely controlled as to launch angle, curvature and power. From there the job of perfecting the golf swing will simply be a matter of repetition.

After spending some time perfecting the new mechanics, until we no longer need to consciously control the body's motion, we will find that some simple changes in the set up will be all we have to do to completely control the flight of the ball .

A WORD OF CAUTION

There are several methods of swinging the club. The left side pull and the rotation swing are but two of many. These different swing types require different body motions to work and their parts are not interchangeable. The components of a swing must fit the swing motion we are trying to make, just as a Ford fender won't fit a Chevy even if they are both yellow and 2003 two-door sedan models.

The swing you are learning here is designed and constructed in a unique way. For it to work it needs to be done in its entirety. It is a recipe for perfect ball striking and just as in any other recipe if we either leave out an ingredient or put too much of an ingredient in we will spoil the result. Mixing some of the swing parts from this book with another swing type is like mixing oil and water. It just does not work. Because of this I implore you to not add anything you learn here to your existing swing. Instead, learn everything about this method as if you were a complete beginner. By doing this you will not be polluting the mix.

If you follow the words and pictures, and do the drills laid out for you in this book, you will be able to build an excellent golf swing in a few months. If you try to take a few parts from this method and add them to your own method you may improve or you may not. As you learn this do not take advice from others. Do not try to incorporate a tip you see in another book or magazine. Stick with the formula and you will attain your goals if you have even a little athletic talent. If you have a lot of talent you may end up being a tour star.

The very best results I have seen in my students come from having a good mental picture of what I want them to do. To that end, the only way that you will get this complete mental picture is by first reading this book as if it were a novel and then studying it as if it were a textbook. Do this before you begin to swing the club and you will learn much more quickly and save yourself considerable frustration.

Everything we do is preceded by a picture in our mind of what we want to accomplish. If you give yourself a good picture of your goal your accomplishments will amaze you.

CHAPTER 3

HOW OUR SWING IS DIFFERENT

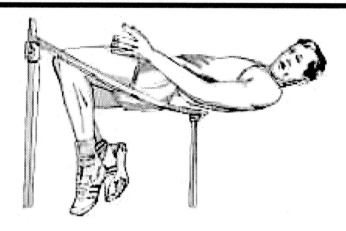

The high jump is a good example of changing the way we think about progress and became a means for improving performance. For decades, the method that virtually all high jumpers used was the straddle method of jumping. Using this method, the jumper kicks one foot up and rolls over the bar face down. The straddle method required leg strength in order to start the jump with the force needed to clear the high jump bar. Many young high jumpers did not have this leg strength and therefore only the naturally strong were successful at the high jump.

Prior to 1968, the record for the high jump remained at 7' 5 3/4" achieved only once by Valerie Brumel in 1963. Dick Fosbury, a high school student from Medford, OR, changed all of this. Dick, like many other high jumpers in the country, learned the method of high jumping taught to him by his coaches and modeled after the usual straddle method. His jumps, though, were mediocre at best. He just couldn't seem to grasp the straddle method of high jumping. Fosbury preferred to use more of a scissors method, popularized by children leaping fences. Eventually, he refined this technique and actually started to jump backwards from the point of take-off. His jump gained international attention and was called the Fosbury Flop.

Fosbury won the gold medal in the 1968 Olympics in Mexico City.

It is now the modern day style employed by almost all high jumpers. More importantly, there are probably better ways to high jump than the Fosbury Flop that people have not thought of yet.

THIS SWING IS DIFFERENT FROM THE COMMON SWING

Golf swings can be compared to several other physical activities such as high jumping or swimming. It is obvious to the eye that there is a large physical difference between some of the swimming strokes such as the breast stroke compared to the Australian crawl. Unlike swimming strokes differences in the golf swing are not always so apparent. Usually these differences are personal mannerisms, or even errors, which have been grooved well enough to allow the player to hit the ball.

Here you will find a swing that has significant differences from the common swing. It is truly an uncommon swing and one that could never be stumbled upon accidentally. This swing is a result of scientific study and research. It has several visual differences, once pointed out, but mostly just looks to the casual observer to be a beautiful and powerful golf swing.

Since the advent of high technology there has been a movement in the teaching of golf toward computer analysis. Modern players have been attempting to emulate the supposed perfect swing installed in a computer data bank. This data has been obtained from video analysis of the swings of some of the top players in the game.

Since almost all of the top teachers of the game are in agreement that the presently agreed upon swing is correct, (although you will get a lot of argument about how to do it) this is the swing that they analyzed. The swings that are on the computer are perfect in that they return the club through the ball in a precise fashion as long as the timing is perfect.

Undeniably some of the top players have practiced these movements and, as close as humanly possible, have perfected them. In Mike Austins's words, "You can perfect imperfection."

In Mike Dunaway's words, "These are high maintenance golf swings. They work well when you practice them a lot and keep the timing required spot on."

For touring professionals, and highly motivated amateurs, swinging this way can produce excellent results so long as the price in practice is paid.

The swing motions described in this book are as different, to what is commonly called perfect, as the old style high jump is different from the Fosbury flop. In the 60's Dick Fosbury popularized a high jump method in which he went over the bar with his back to the bar rather than in the then widely accepted belly roll. When he first started jumping in this manner all of the track and field coaches of the day laughed at him concluding that it was a fluke. Today they all teach his method as the perfect way to high jump. Since this method has been adopted, all high jumpers now use it and the bar has been raised much higher. The method in this book is as radically different as Fosbury's flop. However, it does not look much different unless viewed in extreme slow motion, thus revealing its subtleties.

Ben Hogan introduced the concept of the flat sheet of glass swing plane in his book Five Lessons. This book is considered by many instructors to be their bible and the basis of their teachings. Our concept is very different. In his theory of the swing, the plane was a flat sheet of glass that sat upon the players shoulders that gave the mind a way to picture the swinging of the club. By using this concept he was able to construct his swing and through practice and experimentation made his swing work. His main focus was in the pronation of the left hand on the backswing and supination of the left hand as it returned through the shot. This forearm roll is the ultimate aim of the roller swing mentioned earlier. This theory was ahead of its time, at the time of his book, since nothing else was in print that explained the idea differently.

Mike Austin's concept breaks new ground in the understanding of the plane and shows the complications created in trying to swing the whole club on the Hogan type plane. In the Austin swing we will show that this plane is only the club head plane, not the shaft plane. We will also introduce a new concept we call the "Rotating Plane."

In Austin's concept of the swing the plane rotates with the turning body, while the pronation and supination happen in a different way and at a different point in the swing. The bones in the forearms do not roll over through the hit. Instead they roll under as the wrists swing freely in a hinge-like manner. Due to this unusual release the club swings in a conical fashion. This release action is a major secret of Austin's power and accuracy. It allows the complete transfer of the energy in the speeding club head while keeping the club face square through the hit.

As you will see, as the concept of the rotating plane is explained to you, the only thing in Mike Austin's swing that is ever really on Mr. Hogan's type of plane is the sweet spot of the club head. It never leaves this plane, unlike all other swings.

In the Austin method the right arm folds in a telescoping manner thus keeping the hand plane in the original orbit. The folding of the right arm up, as is commonly done, causes the arms and the club to rise from the shoulders. This action raises the arms and club above the Austin plane in order to swing the whole club on Hogan's plane.

At the top of the backswing our club face and our left wrist are in a position which would be called wrong by the current crop of computer analysts. Our spine position and its motion would be called wrong as we swing the club. These spine positions are similar at address and impact. However, the club head is swinging in an entirely different manner from the hands in the Austin swing than the common swing.

Austin had already formulated his concept of the rotating plane in the 50's but did not publish his work. His ideas were at least 60 years ahead of their time.

Another major work in the golf swing was The Search for the Perfect Swing by two British scientists, Alastair Cochran and John Stobbs published in 1968, who were funded by the Golf Society of Great Britain to gather and publish all that was known about the golf swing at the time. Their book illustrated the swings of many of the top players of the day all of whom used the rolling forearm motion and yet all were quite different.

The work was conducted in a very scientific way and was a huge step forward at the time compared to the other books on teaching that were currently available.

Cochran and Stobbs did a fine job of gathering information, but they could have saved a lot of time and money and better analyzed the motions needed for the perfect swing if they would have simply asked Mike Austin. He was already teaching his method.

In 1969 a work was published by the late Homer Kelly called The Golfing Machine which explained the swing from the viewpoint of a mechanical engineer. This book was extremely complex since he was attempting to show all of the possible combinations one could make while swinging the club.

I am in no way trying to diminish his accomplishments, his work was quite complex, and had he been fortunate enough to meet Mike Austin I am sure he would have been able to instantly grasp the concepts presented here. Undoubtedly his book would have included Austin's method; however, in spite of that omission, the book was still quite enlightening in many areas of the swing. Homer's concept of the 4 barrel swing may have been close, but lacked a concise description. His book and this book will seem a bit over complex to some and every effort has been made to allow people who learn things differently to be able to make use of it's information.

For those who learn visually the photographs and sketches will give a good understanding, for those who also learn through reading, the photos, sketches and captions will add clarity. And, for the scientific types the text will explain the body movements in depth. The body's motion, during the golf swing, is an extremely complex thing to describe and trying to explain something this dynamic with simple thoughts, like feel, will leave the reader with no real knowledge.

Writing a book that describes the feel of a body motion is much like trying to tell someone who has eaten nothing but bananas his whole life what an onion tastes like.

This book will show these concepts together with how the body's design will enable the player to use them in the simplest yet most powerful and repeatable possible way.

Later, we will link the various ideas and body movements together into an understanding of the golf swing, that will at first be a complex collection of related concepts, into a complete and easy to understand mental picture.

We will start with a collection of mind pictures which I will build for you with words, sketches and photos that will show the correct motions of each body part. Your job is to link these images into swing portions and finally link all of the portions together to create a complete mental picture of the golf swing as a full motion. The clarity of this mental picture will create and govern the motions your body makes.

Once the player has this mental picture and is sure that his actions have been practiced and perfected, that knowledge will allow the player to swing with full speed. He will know that if he follows the formula the ball can do nothing except obey his commands. He will have complete control over all aspects of ball flight and will only be limited by his ability to plan the shot correctly.

After over 70 years of research Austin has developed a swing in which the club face is always in perfect alignment to the point in space that anchors the arc of the club head's travel and the points of the compass throughout the arc of its travel. Furthermore, the club head is always on plane and these factors increase the probability factor of the shot's perfection by a significant margin.

When you complete this book you will know exactly where the club face is during every second of the swing motion. Since we will have club head and club face control we can then increase our power through the proper use of the force of our body weight, utilizing leverage and gravity. For perfection, our pivot will anchor the swing-circle-center in space and deliver our power with absolute precision.

To maintain a stationary swing-circle-center we use a pivot motion quite different from the one you probably have learned. It should be studied closely and we will present it early since it is the basis of the controlled motion. This pivot brings the hands and arms and thus the club down plane on the perfect path and is the main power supply in this swing method.

Austin's pivot is visibly different than the comon swing. The head is very still while the lower end of the spine makes a large lateral movement. This is contrary to what some modern instructor's are teaching of trying to rotate the hips, when the hips are moved in a circle we cannot use the weight of the body to gain an advantage. (More on this action in the section on the pivot).

Also, contrary to common instruction is the way we use the wrists and elbows to control the club face and the plane of the club head. The motions we use are almost the exact opposite of what is now accepted as gospel, just as Mr. Fosbury's motion was opposite of what was then the norm.

Instructors for years have said that the straight shot is the hardest shot in golf.

Since their swing required arm roll, this action required perfect timing of the closing club face, to hit a straight shot. Because of that they intentionally caused a draw or a fade hopefully eliminating the opposite curvature. With the Austin swing method, since the arms do not roll, it is no harder to hit a straight shot than any other shot. If you battle a slice, or hook the ball, with this swing you will be able to hit the ball dead straight. The old adage,"The shortest distance between two points is a straight line" is still true.

Another difference with the Austin swing is the manner in which we use the body's weight. As we shift our weight in the pivot we will be using the strength of our strongest muscles exactly where they will do the most good. As an added benefit this pivot will lessen the chances of physical injury, while increasing power output.

The golfer who studies this method will have a blueprint for a perfect swing. This is not to say that the player will always hit perfect shots, since we still have not perfected the mind control that keeps anxiety from hampering our physical actions. However, sports psychologists are closing in on that aspect as well.

This book may be controversial since it takes a different direction from the accepted gospel. It is, however, based on sound scientific logic and if you study this work with an open mind you will likely agree with us.

As the chef said, "The proof is in the pudding".

CHAPTER
4

THE AUSTIN
GRIP

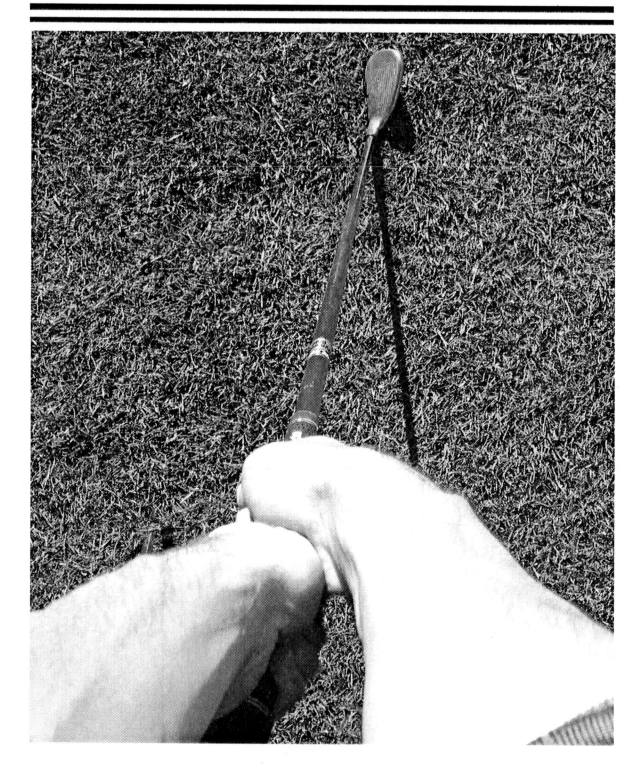

GOLFERS EYE VIEW OF AN EXCELLENT GRIP

THE HANDS AND THE GRIP

The only part of our bodies that touch and thus control the club is our hands. However the hands really should be thought of as being part of the club. The hands themselves do nothing as far as movements are concerned. Their only job is to hold on to the club in a firm yet relaxed fashion and travel as if part of the club. They must not choke the club. By holding on too tight we will not allow the unwinding of the forearms and will impair the motions of the wrists and the elbows that add speed to the club head.

The club head's movements are assisted by gravity combined with centrifugal force. In order for the player to accurately apply his power to the golf ball it is of paramount importance to have a grip that will allow the club head to swing freely as it works in harmony with the arm swing and pivot.

The clubface must return to its original alignments as we swing through the ball, or the shot we get will be inaccurate. The correct grip combined with the free release that you will learn here will automatically give these alignments.

The whole golf club must swing through the ball freely from the wrists like a pendulum would if we are to attain maximum efficiency.

In Mike Austin's words, "We must not impede the pendulum." These words mean that the weighted club head must move the wrists as freely as a well-lubricated hinge. The movement of the wrists however is not a loose or haphazard motion, instead they will be directed by a winding up and unwinding of the forearms in an action that will precisely control the club.

I may describe some wrist and forearm motions as hand actions but understand that any hand motions are actually caused by factors outside the hands, such as the free release of the wrists. However, since we perceive wrist motions to be motions of the hands we will occasionally interchange the terminology.

Since most people are right handed this entire book is written for easy understanding for the majority. If you are left handed please reverse the wording. In the future I plan on making a left handed version available, until then please accept my apology.

For us to properly control the club it is necessary to have a good grip. As the famous instructor Harvey Penick once said, "If you have a bad grip you don't want a good swing." He meant if you ever made a good swing with a bad grip you would get a bad shot.

A bad grip is the mother of a bad swing. The way you grip the club will cause the body to move in a fashion that will allow the grip to return the club squarely into the back of the ball. Even if each must compensate for the mistakes of the other.

If the grip you use is poor, your body's motions must compensate for its inadequacies by making a motion which will generally sacrifice power or reliability. It may also cause the body to injure itself over the long run by placing undue stress on the vertebrae of the back or the joints and tendons of the wrists, shoulders or elbows. The Austin swing is the least injurious way to swing the golf club, and I have no doubt that Mike would still be competing and driving the ball prodigious distances at 93 years of age were it not for the stroke which caused his paralysis.

Fortunately for many players it is possible to make a swing that creates a shot that is acceptable with a bad grip, as long as the swing allows you to get the club on the ball squarely, by making an otherwise unacceptable body motion which then has the effect of canceling each other's negatives.

By having one error cancel another, players with a bad grip or body action are able to hit straight or at least predictable shots. If you notice, I said fortunately since at least 90 percent of golfers are using a grip and swing motion which are suspect to say the least. Surprisingly some touring professionals and low handicap players are in this group, so we know that very good golf can be played with any combination of grip and body movements which together produce powerful predictable results.

In Mike Austin's words,

"They have perfected imperfection."

But at what expense in length of career or physical suffering?

CREATING THE GRIP

Please read this even if you are an accomplished player. You will find some subtle differences and they are vital to this swing action. While learning the proper grip, carefully study the photos since the grip you will be learning is specific to the kind of swinging action taught here.

This grip will be different from the common grip in that it will place the shaft across the base of the fingers of the left hand and not angled across the palm (see photos).

Again this description will be for right-handed players. You lefties are smart enough to simply reverse left and right.

We will start by holding the club in our right hand, at about a 45 degree angle, out in front of the center of our bodies. The butt end of the club should be pointing to the place where your appendix would be if your appendix were on the left side of your body instead of the right side.

(Finally science finds a use for the appendix).

Here the club is held in the right hand with the shaft pointing just inside the left hip. The score lines on the club face should be vertical.

At this point we want our right hand holding the shaft of the club some twelve or fourteen inches above the grip. The shaft should be angled up enough to point the score lines on the face vertical to the ground. The leading edge of the club face should be on the center line of the body. When the club is held in this fashion it will enable us to place the left hand on the club easily.

Place the entire length of the thumb all of the way to the heel pad directly on the top center line of the shaft so that 1/2 inch of the butt end of the grip protrudes from the hand, now simply close your fingers.

If you turn your hand so you would be looking at your palm, you should find your hand looking like a fist with your thumb extended vertically. A small amount of angle across the palm is acceptable.

To apply the correct right hand grip, hook the two center fingers of your right hand while keeping the index finger and pinky extended, the fingers will be placed under the shaft as if you were carrying a bucket in them. The shaft rests on the center bone of the fingers, (be careful not to get the shaft too close to the palm) and slide the right hand toward the left hand until the right hand ring finger collides with the left index finger.

Now simply close the right pinky over and into the notch between the left index finger and the middle finger.

When you close the right hand the left thumb base knuckle will snuggle nicely into the pocket formed at the base of the right palm. The base knuckle should be exactly where the point of the arrow is. It should feel very comfortable in this position, and will give maximum legerage.

The significant differences in this grip are that the club is directly across the base of the fingers of the left hand and the left hand will be in (what is commonly called) a slightly weaker position. This position is anything but weak. It will prove to be the strongest grip you can possibly have since the wrists will be able to rotate the club beneath the forearms with maximum wrist-cock both going back and going through. If the grip is in any other position the movements of the wrists will be limited in one of the two directions.

The grip is designed this way so that we may rotate the shaft under the hands and forearms as we release the club so that the right hand does not have to roll over the left hand. In the swing you are learning, the right hand will pass between the left hand and the ball since that is where it is on the grip.

After the grip is formed we will be able to perform the conical chip as shown in the sketches and photos beginning on page 44. This chip is the key to understanding a different way of releasing the club. This release is designed to take full advantage of the wrist's range of motions while at the same time controlling the club face by eliminating the rolling shaft. Now lets see how it differs in its use compared to the standard swing as we learn the Austin release.

This grip is similar to, but slightly different than, the Vardon grip. It is the Austin grip. For the Austin swing to perform at peak efficiency this is the grip we recommend. The thumb of the left hand must be buried in the pocket of the right palm, it should not be visible.

CHAPTER 5

THE CONICAL ACTION OF THE CLUB

WHY THE CLUB SWINGS DIFFERENTLY

One of the largest visible differences between this swing and the other types of swings, that have been taught for decades, is that through impact we do not use a motion which will cause the club face to rotate around the shaft. The goal of all golf swings is to make the club return perfectly through the ball. Yet today's golf instructors, at every level, teach a swing action that alters the relationship between the club face and the ball. This causes the player to need to undo these alterations on the downswing. (See photos pages 61-66).

The commonly accepted wrist and arm movements cause the club face to revolve around the shaft while the wrists cock up and down. At the same time, the arms also rise and lower from the shoulder sockets. These things change the clubs relationship to the body and the ball by changing planes. If that's not complex enough due to the roll of the forearms the club face opens and closes.

In Austin's swing we do none of the above.

Austin calls swinging with the commonly used swing, playing Russian roulette since the player is never really sure if his timing will be perfect enough to produce a square contact. In the Austin swing we will maintain the club-ball alignments set at address, simplifying solid contact and preserving shot predictability, yet hitting with increased power.

By using what we call the counter rotation of the forearms we will be able to keep the club face correctly aligned with the ball rather than allowing it to roll open. Rolling open is what happens naturally as the right arm bends at the elbow, if we don't compensate for it with this slight forearm counter rotation. By today's standards "naturally occcuring" is a synonym for good. Here though it can be done without. Remember the plague is also "naturally occuring."

Aside from not using the rotating shaft action, following are some of the other differences. We will not allow the club head to travel off plane by the unique way we will use the combined actions of our elbow, wrist and shoulder joints.

This action we call the tromboning of the arms since the movements resemble the movements of playing the trombone. You will also find as the club swings through impact we will allow the wrists to hinge sideways, a movement which has been considered taboo for years.

HOW TO KILL THE BALL

As you will soon see, within every full swing there exists a little shot. If we can learn to control our hands and forearms with this shot then the arm swing battle is half won and we will be correctly controlling the lower half of our arms. It is the control of the club face with the forearms that allows the wrists to freely release the energy created by the rest of the levers into the ball. Our golf swing, going down is exactly the reverse of the moves we make going back. Because of this, the smallest shot is only the last part of the biggest shot. Thus, each larger shot is simply a little larger piece of the full golf swing.

The wonderful thing about learning the swing this way is that it will instantly improve your chipping accuracy since it keeps the club head and face traveling in a straight line directly away from and back toward the target. In other words, in this area the club head is traveling straight at the target as the club face is releasing down under and up. This action will make it easy to hit our chips straight and with the right power and trajectory.

This kind of precision is exactly what we need to happen in all full shots. Only through learning this movement, starting from the chip, will we be able to correctly use the lever assembly to its maximum potential when we are pounding drivers.

The precision we learn here will enable us to control the height and curvature of all shots with all clubs and is the key to ball striking excellence. The arm actions will be discussed later in more detail in the chapter on the rotating plane and the conical action of the club head. However, for now, just learn and practice the little shot so that by the time you get to the other sections you will have laid the foundation for them.

In the photo series (following pages) notice that the shaft of the club is below the arms and that in this position it is also under the hands. If we swung the club head, while using our hands in a cranking manner, it would be easy to see that as the shaft passes beneath the arms, the club head moves quite a long distance with the club face not rolling open or closed but instead remaining square to the flight line. This action is much like cranking a scissors jack. This cranking action of the hands is a portion of the release action and is controlled by the unwinding forearms. When the other actions of the arms are understood this will make more sense.

THE CONICAL RELEASE

In the Austin method, we will learn a release that keeps the face of the club both traveling along the line and square to it much longer.

To accomplish this we will learn a unique way to swing the club head through the ball. In the Austin method our club shaft will be rotating in the exact opposite direction of the common release.

We will begin to learn this release with a chip shot that I call the little shot. In this shot we will learn to swing the club head through the ball while controlling the club face with the right forearm.

But before we do, let's see why this is important to learn.

A WEIGHT SWINGING FROM A TACK IN THE CEILING WOULD PRODUCE A CONE

For those of you having trouble here's a little something for you. No, its not a dunce cap, its a cone. Bring it along as you will need it soon.

The above sketch shows how a weight would swing from a tack in the ceiling. Notice that the weight is swinging in a circle but the overall result is a cone. So it is with the club, since the actions of our wrists and forearms will swing the club in an entirely different manner, in the Austin method, than in the standard golf swing. Our club head travels in a circle, but the shaft follows a cone.

This release action is very free and extremely accurate. Again, we will learn how to do it by starting with a shot I call the little shot. This shot will train the hands and forearms to swing the club in a conical action. This action will cause a perfectly controlled circular arc of the club head within the full swing.

THE ACTIONS OF THE HANDS

Due to the design of the wrist and forearm, the hand can move as if the wrist were a horizontal axle no matter what angle the hand is at relative to the forearm. In the sketches below you can see how the wrist can raise or lower the hand without changing the position of the forearm bones.

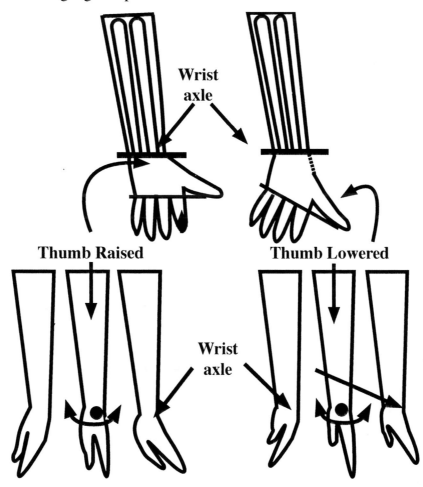

The hands on the left show the thumb in the lowered position, the hands on the right show the hands in the raised position. Due to the wrist's ability to rotate around the wrist axle the hands can release the club under the wrists regardless of the condition of the hand relative to the forearm. This also allows the hands to work in a car crank manner as we release the club as you will see on the following pages. Also, due to this ability, we will be able to swing all clubs with the same arm action. The steep shaft angle of the wedges or the flatter shaft angle of the driver and long irons will not require any change in our action.

The Car Crank Action of the Wrists

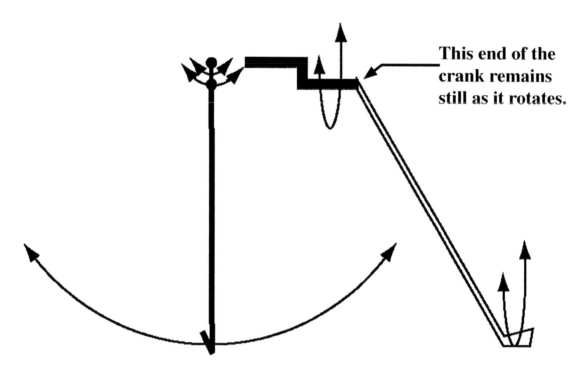

This end of the crank remains still as it rotates.

The sketch above shows a club with a crank handle, since our right hand is below the left when we use our wrists in the direction of the arrows the club head swings down under and up, the perfect way to attain square, solid contact. Since the right hand wrist axle is below the left hand axle, and also because the wrists work around the axles regardless of the hand angles, the hands can work like a crank as they release. This action keeps the club face square to the flight line, increasing accuracy.

The radius from the left wrist axle to the club head determines club head distance of travel. The radius of the right wrist, from the wrist axle to the base of the fingers, rotates under the left wrist axle just as a crank would. This type of release both increases the space where the club face is square to the target and at the same time frees-up the swinging club head. The club must freely swing beneath the wrist axles just as a pendulum does beneath a clock. For this to occur the arms must relax and allow gravity to swing the pendulum.

The way we set our wrist angles and wind-up our forearms as we make our backswing will control the correct position of the club face as the club reacts to centrifugal force and gravity as it swings through impact.

When we use our hands to move the club in a cranking fashion the club head swings in a conical action. By swinging this way, our club face passes through the ball in a more precise and powerful manner. As you will learn later this movement keeps the club face on plane and square to the ball throughout the entire swing. It also allows us to maintain the correct hand plane and orbit thus simplifying the actions.

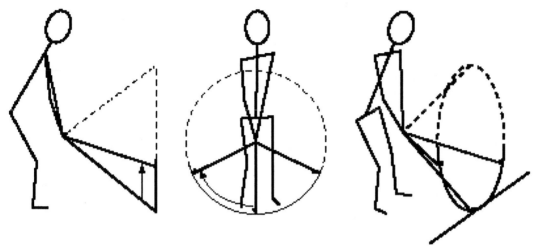

If a picture is worth a thousand words, here are three thousand.

The motions you see in the sketches on this page are a result of the car crank hand wrist and forearm actions. These we must learn and practice in the little shot. The conical action is plainly visible and must occur in all larger shots as well even though it will be invisible there. This action will only send the ball about ten yards with a sand wedge.

In this shot, since the elbows are not involved, the point of the triangle formed by the arms and shoulders remains in the center of the body and does not move. This shot is done with the wrists and forearms and a tiny bit of elbow movement. Notice, also, that the angle between the left arm and shaft does not change, since the wrists did not cock up and cause the club head to change planes. Due to this, the club head returns precisely to the ball. In the Austin swing the wrists never cock vertically as that action causes the club head to change planes.

Remember the elbows as well as hands must move in all shots LONGER than this one.

The following pages present a photo series that should be studied while reviewing the proceeding pages of text. Any confusion should be explained. If not, don't worry as the mind picture is still developing and will soon be clear.

I want you to see the spoon in the photo above as the face of your golf club. The next few photos will show what we do and do not want to do.

In this photo the spoon has been turned away from the ice cream and opened, this is what the common hand motion does with the club face. As you will see in the next pictures this complicates future moves.

The palm of the hand has turned face up, thus supinating the spoon. This will necessitate the reverse motion back through the ball and, thus, a roll of the shaft must be timed by rolling the forearms. From here the left hand, as Hogan taught, which now would have the palm facing down must supinate (turn the palm up and over) in order to re-square the blade. (see photo next page)

Here we see the results of the pronating spoon. The ice cream is not going up, it's heading for points unknown. This movement works when well timed, but can also produce a low hook, if mis-timed. Hogan compensated for this by weakening his grip and bowing the left wrist through impact. Austin's method allows for the complete club head release without fear of the hook. With the common swing action, because the forearms are rolling the club face closed, if the player fully releases the wrists there is a good chance of hooking the shot.

Here we go again, only this time we will use the Austin release.

As the spoon or club face retreats from the ball notice how the face turns under, this is counter rotation, and is a small and slow move that keeps the club face aligned with the ball or the spoon aligned with the ice cream.

Our spoon has returned square to the ice cream as the hands reversed the motion that they made on the way back. This unwinding action of the forearms happens naturally when we are hitting full shots as the wound up muscles relax and seek center.

Here we see the spoon as the right hand supinates and we see the ice cream getting on top of the spoon. This type of release is good off any kind of lie, especially out of the rough, since it goes down under and up while the toe and heel of the club travel together rather than the common toe going faster than the heel roll over type of release. Because of this release, the Austin swing allows a hard hit with the hands and arms without the fear of the unwanted hook. Remember, the spoon must get under the ice cream. I did not say to pick the ball clean, a divot should be taken to insure solid contact.

CHAPTER 6

THE LITTLE SHOT

THE UNDERSTANDING OF THE CONICAL CLUB
ACTION BEGINS WITH A SHOT
I CALL THE LITTLE SHOT

We start with the hands in this phase of learning the Austin method with the little shot. This shot is to be learned and practiced while you are reading the rest of the book. It is the winding up and releasing action of the forearms. It is what the hands must do in all full shots, to swing and control the club. Later, when we add the rest of the arm swing and the pivot motions, we will already have control of the release. In order to control the face of the club as it travels rapidly around the body we will also use this exact forearm motion. At first it will seem to be totally wrong, but later when you blend it with the other Austin arm movements you will see that it is perfectly correct.

Now that we have had our ice cream we can use the cone to show you how the release works. We will begin by learning how to cock the right wrist while, at the same time, we counter rotate the shaft under with our left forearm. These are the earliest movements in the backswing arm actions and since our downswing is the exact reverse of our backswing, as we hit they come last. We will also be using this exact action in our chipping.

The learning of the arm movements will be broken into three phases in order to simplify the learning process. By separating the phases we will be able to see each movement in great detail. The better our mental picture is of the motions, then the better we will make them. As Austin said in his first video tape, "Golf is mental imagery." We start with the chip, which is also the full swing release.

The release is the actions of the hands that allow the club to swing freely from the wrists and release through the impact area just as the spoon did with the ice cream. We will do this without conscious control and yet it will be totally controlled as to direction and alignment.

Learning this at this point in the book gives you time to train your forearms in the motions they make to control the club face through impact before you begin hitting the ball hard. It is much easier this way. By the time you finish reading the book you will be ready for the other parts of the arm swing. You will find the other two phases of the arm action after the chapter about the pivot. Please do not skip ahead.

As in the photos on the following pages, if you hold the club in your hands and waggle the club in a cranking and cocking motion so that the club face does not rotate you will see that this is a much more accurate way to strike the ball. It eliminates the timing of the roll and we gain the use of the wrists to both add power and to control the height of the shot. It is easy to get the feel of how the wrists hinge when we swing the club this way.

Moving the wrists in this fashion has long been considered a major fault in the swing as it is commonly being taught. The exact language used to describe this action is the breaking down of the wrists. We call the idea of holding the left wrist flat and only allowing a wood chopping action of the hands, combined with a forearm roll, an unnecessary complication and a potential error lurking and always ready to show its ugly face when the pressure is on.

The smallest shot is only the last part of the biggest shot. Each larger shot is simply a little larger piece of the full golf swing. In order to learn this unique motion of the club head we must begin with understanding what the club head does as it travels away from and back through the ball. The ice cream photos were carefully posed to get this idea across, please go back and study them again as you contemplate the words about the little shot.

The counter rotation will at first seem as if we are creating a complication, when the exact opposite is true. As one of my students once said, "it is counter intuitive but it sure works." It is the beginning of the motions we will be using as we later make larger swings.

As you will see in the photos and sketches the club head will not immediately swing inside the flight line. Instead, it will go up and back directly above it.

The club head moves in a conical action relative to the wrists. There will be more on the conical action later. On page 46 the sketch shows the portion of the cone we use. The actions of the hands that produce this cone are similar to a cranking motion.

These photos show that any rolling action of the shaft does not advance the blade, instead it opens and closes it.

Here we see the hit movement of the right wrist that would advance the club head and, as you can see, it does not revolve the shaft. This release action of the right wrist is caused by the most powerful of the forearm muscles giving us power and accuracy.

PHOTO #1

The little club, shown here, is a fine training aid and lets you see just what the movements of the forearms and wrists do and give us instant feed back for the correct feel. The black arrow shows the direction of the counter rotation movement of the shaft. This is not a misprint. We will turn the shaft in the direction of the arrow, just like loosening a screw with a screwdriver.

PHOTO #2

In this photo the club has been swung back by a turning under of the left wrist and a slight counter roll of the left forearm. The move feels like you tucked your left pinky knuckle under and, correctly done, produces the wrist and club position you see. The shaft is 45 degrees to the ground and the left wrist is slightly bowed and thus cocked. This is the combined counter rotation and wristcock. The movements could be described as the combined crank and hinge movements of the wrist. This is what the hands do in the stick figure sketches. Close examination shows the left wrist to be slightly bowed. If the muscles just relaxed, the weight of the swinging club head would allow the free swinging club head to return squarely to, and through, the ball. Our golf swing is exactly the reverse on the down swing as the actions we made going back.

PHOTO #3

If, in the previous photo, you had the right hand on the club, the wrist would have been able to cock straight back and into the optimum hitting position. The left wrist would now be in the same position as in picture #2.

It is interesting to note that this is how the right wrist looks at the end of the full release for a left-handed person. For the right handed players release see next photo.

PHOTO #4

It is easy to visualize what the right hand would have had to do to return the left hand to this position. What the hands do on the way back, they undo on the way through. The right hand would have cranked under the left hand and would be in the same condition (in reverse) as the left wrist is in the photo on page 57. Notice that the wrist that is bowed appears to have moved less than the wrist that is cupped. The left wrist in this photo has released 45 degrees, the same amount that it cocked in photo #2.

THE ARM SHAFT ANGLE

On the previous pages the little club revealed the wrist movements critical to this way of swinging. On the following page is a photo that relates to the angle formed at address between the left arm and the club shaft. This angle is felt to be a constant. We do not change it by raising the thumbs. It is important to understand that our wrists work opposite to the way the wrists work in the conventional swing. The conventional swing maintains the wrist angle sideways by allowing no flapping of the wrists and instead cocks the wrists vertically in a chopping fashion. This action requires the club head to roll around the shaft.

In the Austin wrist action the wrists do not cock vertically. They move the club head sideways to the arm-shoulder triangle and thus eliminate the club head roll and the changing of the plane caused by the raising of the thumbs and the arms.

Unlike all other swings which cock the club head up with a vertical movement, we will cock the club head with a horizontal movement thus keeping the club head at the bottom of the arc it makes around the wrists. This will cause the face of the club to always be square to this arc as it releases through impact.

The photos on the pages that follow (62-66) show the complications caused by the hand and arm movements as they are done in the common swing.

ARM SHAFT
ANGLE

This is the arm-shaft angle. We do not conciously change this angle at any point in the Austin swing. It does change slightly, when it is a long way from the ball, but we will never attempt to change it.

The white line in this photo shows the club properly soled, it is also on plane. As you will see in later chapters the plane in this book is described differently.

This photo shows that cocking the club vertically lifts the clubhead above the plane. If at any point in the golf swing your thumbs rise above the top edge of your forearms you will have changed the arm shaft angle and thus altered the plane of the clubhead.

If the player raises the thumbs and thus the club head vertically he must then roll the left arm to the right from the shoulder socket to compensate for this motion thus getting the club head back on Hogan's plane. Unfortunately it has also rotated the shaft.

This complicates the motion since now the hosel of the club is facing the ball rather than the club face requiring a return roll of the shaft to square it back up. No matter where the club face opens in the swing, it must be returned to square at impact, this is the built in potential error of the roller swing action. *Since our player made two moves in the backswing he will now have to un-do these positions by reversing the two movements as he swings down to get the club head back squarely to the ball.* **Doing this requires perfect timing.**

In the photo on the facing page the player raised the club head off plane and compensated with arm roll. In the photo above he has returned it to the ball with the correct amount of downward uncocking of the wrists, but without enough unroll. By doing this he would shank or slice the ball. If the return move had enough unrolling, but not the correct uncocking, he would hit a fat, thin, or bladed, shot. The slice may be useful if planned for, but in the Austin method we would go about creating it differently.

Here our player has returned the club to square but too much uncock has caused a fat shot.

The following photo series illustrates the club's action when the wrists are used with the correct forearm counter rotation. If you are swinging the club head by cranking the shaft in a conical fashion, it will stay square and travel straight back and up. Reversing the actions will cause the club head to return straight down the flight line and up. Do not bend the elbows as you do this drill or you will pull the club inside the line.

In this photo, the counter-rotation of the forearms is started, it is a very small move of the left forearm from the elbow. To do it, turn the left pinky knuckle slightly under. This will take the heel of the club back with the toe as you cock the right wrist straight back. If this is done correctly, the club face will remain square with both clubs and will go straight back and rise directly between them. This is the human equivalent of the stick figure sketch on page 46.

Here the club head has reached the limit of the hands-only travel. The club shaft is now 45 degrees to the right of center and 45 degrees to the ground. Notice that the club head is still square to the direction and has only risen, not rotated. The feel is that the club made about 1/8 of the conical action. In the full swing, because of the elbow movements, the cone will be larger. The club head in the full swing will describe the lower half of a full cone shaped arc, relative to the body, but will be invisible to observers.

As the forearms unwind the club head swings down under and up. As you can see, the ball has no choice but to go straight. It is important as we practice these little shots to keep the arm-shaft angle constant. Your club should be traveling in the lower portion of the conical action as shown in the sketch on page 46.

This is as far as the hands release the club head, again the shaft is 45 degrees to the ground and 45 degrees to the flight line. This is the exact hand and wrist action we will use in a full swing and is solely controlled by the wrists and forearms. Practice this shot well and it will reward you with many chip-ins and good control of the releasing club head later.

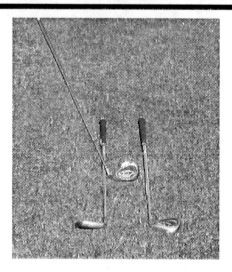

When we make the left-hand, turn-under move by tucking the left pinky knuckle as we cock the right wrist straight back we should attain this club head position. Notice that the club face is de-lofting and remaining in line and above the flight line. Notice that if we were in front of a left-handed person chipping instead of in back of a right-handed person the club face would have increased in loft after it passed through the ball.

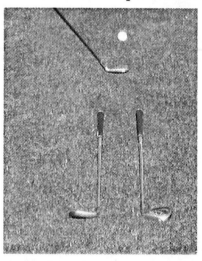

Here we see the right-handed chip. The club face has hit the ball with normal loft, but now it has more loft as the club completes the counter rotation. In this photo it is even more obvious. In mirror image view this would be the lefty's beginning of the backswing move and the club face would be de-lofted.

Our movement makes the club head release down, under and up and is much more accurate. It is not a scooping action, since the club head is swinging down and striking the ball just before it reaches the bottom of the release arc.

CHAPTER 7

THE STANCE

A PERFECTLY MEASURED STANCE

UNDERSTANDING AND LEARNING THE STANCE

The stance is the place from where we start the golf swing. It locates our distance from the ball, positions our bodies to deliver the blow correctly down and through the ball and locates the swing circle center. The caption below the picture on the facing page reads "A PERFECTLY MEASURED STANCE." From the stance position that Jaacob is in he could strike the ball efficiently with either hand if he chose to make a one-handed swing.

I chose those words carefully because, in our method, we are measuring the location of the swing-circle-center very accurately. We use the club as a measure to position our bodies in a precise manner, so we can pivot away from, and back through the shot with maximum power and still be able to maintain the swing-circle-center in its exact location.

In the Austin Method the swing-circle-center remains, anchored in its original location until well after the club head has hit the ball. It is very important to swing around a fixed center since it will make consistent impact easier and will allow us to generate more club head speed. A simple way to see the importance of the still head is to twirl a weight on a string. Take a 1-ft long piece of string and tie a weight of about 1 or 2 ounces to it, (a key ring works nicely) and make large rotary motions with your right wrist, you will see that the keys move in a circle with a moving center and do not move particularly fast. If you make smaller and smaller loops with your hand, the weight will gain speed and when your hand is making tiny circles the weight will be literally zooming around.

The concept of swinging the key ring around the hand is very important in this swing method as you will see later when the arm action is added to the pivot.

As a matter of fact, the feel of twirling the weight is almost exactly the feel of twirling the club head in the full swing. Our club will be twirled from the right wrist and elbow and the club head will zing around as quickly as those keys.

The swing we will be learning generates massive power and so the machine must be stable in order to utilize it. A powerful swing will create powerful errors, and a moving swing circle center is an error waiting to happen. More will follow, dealing with stabilizing the swing-circle-center, in the section on the pivot.

By using the club to measure our distance from the ball we can precisely locate and set the stance. The correct stance gives us the measurement from the swing-circle-center to the ball we must maintain if we expect consistent contact. It also allows us to use our leg and trunk muscles to shift and rotate our body's weight, around and through the shot, while remaining in balance.

The correct positioning of the properly fitted club to the ball and the ground is our starting point for all iron and fairway wood shots. When we set the club on the ground properly we are able to move our bodies into the correct position relative to the club rather than trying to position the club somehow into whatever space is left between the body and the ball after we take our stance.

The forward (toward-the-ball) spine angle is one of the angles we must learn to set as we take our stance. The correct forward tilt angle is about 30 degrees or 1:00 o'clock. Each player will have to determine his own spine angle based on the lengths of his arms, legs and spine, as the following photo series will show.

This angle is a relative one since, in the swing you are learning here, we will cause the lower end of the spine to move laterally to the right when the weight transfers to the right foot as we turn away from the ball. This toward-the-ball spine angle remains constant, while the lower end of the spine slides laterally right and left as the weight shifts from one leg to the other as we make the swing.

It is this lateral movement of the lower end of the spine that allows the swing-circle-center to remain fixed in space as the body weight shifts -- first, from the center to the right foot and then back past center to the left foot as the ball is struck. This lateral sliding hip action also causes a tremendous windup of the internal muscles of the trunk.

The photos and the captions will show this in great detail in the section devoted to the weight shift. In that chapter you will learn two drills that perfect this action.

Take the proper grip on the club while standing erect, with locked knees. Lower the arms until they touch the body. At this point the shaft should be pointing roughly at the inside corner of the top of the left hip, at belly-button height.

Next, tilt forward as if taking a bow, *KEEPING THE KNEES LOCKED.* This sets the angle of your spine by first tilting it forward toward the ball from the hip sockets. As you do this, hold the torso militarily erect. This will protect the spine. Keep the knees locked straight until the club almost touches the ground. Keep the weight evenly distributed on both feet. This will cause the derriere to counter balance the upper body weight (see photos following pages).

Now, to complete the lowering of the club, unlock the knees slightly, but keep them as close to straight as possible. Bend the knees just a tiny bit, too much will lower the head. Do not reach out with your arms to reach the ball.

Take baby steps until the ball is in the center of the club face. Check yourself with mirrors; try for perfection.

This photo shows the forward tilt while not yet bending the knees, this makes the derriere go back which counter-balances the weight of the head, arms and club. The dotted line shows how the body counter-balances; the weight on one side of the line equals the weight on the other. It also sets the spine angle at the correct 30 degrees from vertical (white lines). The weight should be equal on each foot and centered between the balls of the feet and the heels. Notice that the arms do not hang straight down they angle out from the body by a few degrees. The hands hang directly above the toes. Here the clubhead is still two or three inches above the ground.

In this photo Jaacob has lowered the club head to the ground by the knee actions descrbied below and as he did this, he removed his right hand from the club. With the right hand off the club, re-align your chest with your hips in order to be sure that the chest and shoulders are properly aligned. This subtle but important move keeps your body alignment perfect. The distance we measure at address (arrow) must not change. Starting from a correctly measured stance makes every action of the swing easier.

As you reach for the club with your right hand, simultaneously straighten the left knee slightly as you flex the right knee a tiny amount. This movement will slide and open the hips a small amount laterally left and add some weight to the left heel. The weight on the right foot should move slightly to the inside of the ball of the foot without raising the heel. This movement also slightly lowers the right shoulder, thus allowing the right hand to grasp the club while keeping the shoulder square to the spine. The right shoulder lowers correctly because the lower end of the spine moved left with the pelvis caused by the knee movements.

In this photo Jaacob has returned the right hand to the club and has allowed the lower end of the spine to slide a little left, as he flexed his right knee. He is in perfect balance and can swing all out without fear of moving his head.

Contrary to the common stance, his left knee is almost perfectly straight rather than flexed. In the Austin Method the height of the swing-circle-center always remains the same since we always have one leg or the other straight, just as you naturally have the leg that is holding up your weight straight during the act of walking. This is the perfect stance. Starting from the perfect stance is the easiest way to make a perfect backswing, an important factor in solid ball-striking. It is attention to details like these that creates precision.

HOW TO KILL THE BALL

Here Jaacob is in the exact position as on the facing page; he has not moved a muscle, the right knee is bent a tiny amount while the left leg is straight. His stance is very square to where he wants the ball to go and the ball can go nowhere else without a big mistake in the motion.

As the right hand goes back on the club, the knees should not move more than one or two inches. As they move, the hips will tilt slightly as the left shoulder goes up with the lengthening left leg and the right shoulder lowers with the shortening right leg. The hips will also turn open slightly and slide laterally left a small amount. The right side of the torso will shorten slightly thereby lowering the right shoulder. These actions allow the right hand to grab the club.

What makes this knee and spine movement the right size is the right hand's ability to grasp the club with no movement above the waist. The lowering of the right hand into position is only caused by the flexing of the right knee and the lateral slide of the hips, do not over do this. Correctly done, this tilts the lower end of the spine. The shoulders, relative to the spine, will not move at all.

The right hand only has to be lowered, by the above moves, about two to three inches depending upon the size of your hands. As the right knee makes that tiny flex the hips slide laterally left enough to point the lower end of the spine right at the center of your left heel. The "T" formed by your spine and shoulders must still be a letter "T" not twisted into a bit of an italic caused by a shoulder move, as in *"T."*

In this photo we see the ball placed directly between the feet. We recommend that you learn to hit the ball in this location with all clubs up to the 9 iron. This is the starting point in learning ball placement and is where the ball will be played with these clubs for a standard-height shot.

The "T" formed by the spine and shoulders is square, showing that the lowering of the right hand was done by the knees and the slight lateral slide of the hips. The arrows show the movement of the "T," caused only by the movements of the knees, as the right hand was applied.

HOW TO KILL THE BALL

In this photo we see the ball played more forward in the stance. This is the 3 iron. The ball is about 3 inches forward of center for standard shots, since each club longer than the 9 iron is played a half inch forward of the next lower club's placement. With practice this will soon be done naturally.

When we adjust our body to the correctly soled club by allowing the club's angles to dictate our body's location we will be able to make a swing that is virtually the same with all clubs. The only difference being the slight difference of the angle of the wrists at address.

When you have your body in the correct position relative to the ball, you will find that it is much easier to hit the long irons. We will not have to change anything we do in the swing, to hit standard shots with any club, except position the body correctly to the ball. After you learn the swing, you will want to learn the shots that are not standard. These shots require a different ball position. The advanced shots will be covered in my next book.

 In this photo we see the body in the same exact position for both the 9 iron and the three iron. The club may change, but the stance of the body does not. The stance and body movements in the Austin swing are the same for all clubs.

CHAPTER
8
THE GATE

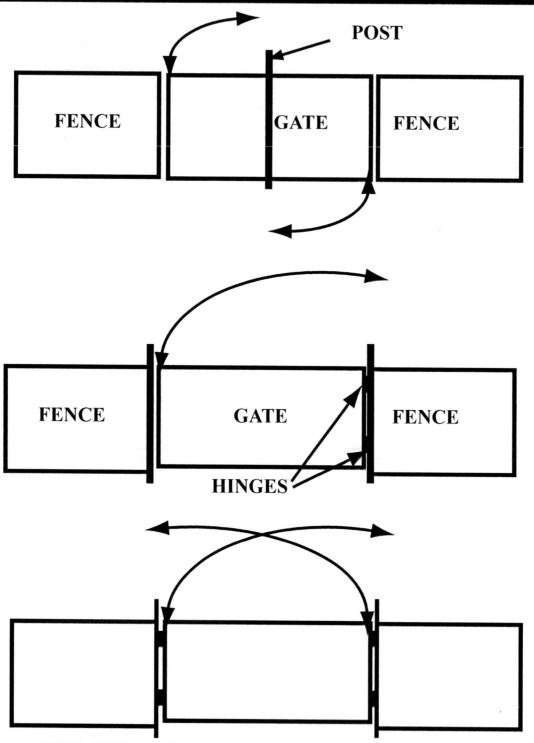

POST

FENCE   GATE   FENCE

FENCE   GATE   FENCE

HINGES

THE SWING OF THE GATE IN THIS SKETCH DEPENDS UPON WHICH HINGE PINS WE PULL

THE GATE

This section describes a gate-like movement we will be using in our golf swing. This motion refers to the shifting of the weight and the revolving of the torso.

Over the centuries, man has invented many kinds of gates for various purposes. As we study the pivot, we should understand the actions of several different types in order to better understand the way we use our bodies for the most efficient mechanical advantage.

The first style of gate is like a revolving door: a central post with one half of the door swinging into one room or field and the opposite half revolving in the opposite direction into the other room. (Top sketch facing page).

This type of motion is advocated by some teachers whose students, when given this swing concept, attempt to make a turn as if a huge nail were driven through their heads and down through their spines and into the ground like the gate in the top sketch. This image causes poor leg action since this body turn does not consider the fact that the human spine enters the pelvis in the center but the legs attach to the pelvis at the outboard ends. Attempting to turn around this imaginary nail brings many complications to the pivot, none of them good. So, without entering into a very complex description of all the things that could and do go wrong when trying this movement, I will just say that the very best thing that could happen is likely not to be very good.

This motion puts the legs into a position where they cannot efficiently apply their effort and, most likely, this action will cause the head to move. Movement of the head turns the stationery ball into a moving target (it is much easier to hit a target if the target and the shooter are both still); if either one of the two should move, accuracy declines. It is much easier to hit a target with a rifle while standing still than when riding a galloping horse. We could rotate in this manner if we had only one leg directly below the spine but we have two and the Austin Method uses them both in the most efficient manner.

Another type of gate has hinges on one end and can make a wide arc, as does the gate in the center sketch. If we were to hinge the gate at the opposite end, it would then make the opposite arc.

The bottom sketch on page 88, shows a gate hinged at both ends. This gate would be unable to move since both sides are firmly attached, but if we pulled the hinge pins from one side, we could then pivot the gate open in a wide arc in one room or field. We could then slam shut the gate, and if we put the hinge pins back in the hinges, while removing the opposite set of hinge pins, the gate could then swing on the other post back out and around into the same room or field.

A gate must be supported on a post or a wall in such a way so as to allow it to swing in its desired arc without hitting the ground. If the post were not straight, up and down, the gate would either dig into the ground or rise above it. If the post were leaning out from the fence, the gate would hit the ground. To allow it to swing, we could cut off the bottom of the gate but that would not be the best way. The best way would be to have the post placed perfectly vertical (assuming level ground). This gate would also swing very freely (assuming we had well-oiled hinges). The body pivots on the legs the same way, the leg must be straight and vertical for the pelvis to rotate correctly.

In the Austin pivot, the left side of the body turns in toward the ball on the posted right leg as we swing back. The right side of the body swings out toward the ball on the downswing so that we are hitting the ball with the full weight of our bodies behind, and turning into, the shot.

This is the foundation for the understanding of the pivot. The next chapter will give more insight. Don't be worried if these last few words leave you a little lost. The sketches and photos coming soon will clarify all of it for you.

CHAPTER
9
THE PIVOT

The text in this section will be much easier to understand when combined with the following sketches and photo series. Read through it and then study the photos. After that, come back and read it again, while paging back and forth between the correct photos relative to the text. The better the mind can grasp the motions, the easier it will be to do them. The drills that come later in the book will perfect the motions. You will greatly increase your power if you combine the knowledge with the repitition of the correctly done actions.

THE AUSTIN PIVOT

To hit the ball farther we must hit the ball solidly. The Austin pivot provides a stable swing-circle-center for solid contact. It also uses the maximum power available from the legs, internal trunk muscles and weight of the body. The pivot also uses the body as a large lever assembly. Correctly executed, the backswing pivot positions the leg and trunk muscles so they can be used in their most efficient manner as we return through the ball

To attain rock-solid impact, we must have precise contact between the club and the ball combined with speed and acceleration through the hit. To this end, we must first address our ability to maintain a perfectly stable swing-circle-center. This point is approximately one inch in front of the largest vertebra in the back of our neck. The center of our swing rotation is not in the middle of our necks, it is four inches behind the front of our necks.

Keeping this point still in space will locate the center of the upper rotating lever assembly, the shoulders, arms and club. Done correctly, this guarantees that the club returns to the exact location from whence it started. Assuming, of course, that the angles created between the arms and the club return the club head to the same location we measured, to when we took our address. Later, we will deal with our arms' ability to increase club head speed through the previously measured location at impact.

To partly understand the pivot, we can look to the actions of a bowler. A big strong man could stand right at the foul line and, using only the strength of his arm and upper body, he could throw the ball down the lane. Let's say he rolls the ball at 25 mph. To increase the speed of the ball, he retreats several yards and runs up to the foul line while throwing the ball. If he could attain the speed of 8 mph, the ball would now be rolling at 33 mph. This is a 25% increase.

The same is true for the golfer. The better we can coil up behind the ball, and gain body speed with the pivot, the farther the arms and hands can hit the ball. To do this the legs must run, and the hips must tilt.

Unlike most other swing methods, the downswing pivot is not an attempt at making a rotary motion with the chest. Instead it is a lateral tilt and slide of the hips as we transfer the weight from the right leg to the left leg. This hip tilt and slide is done by the actions of the feet and knees which shift the weight laterally. Assisting and helping to power this move are the powerful internal trunk muscles which shorten the sides of the body. Shortening the sides of the body tilts the pelvis relative to the spine. This action in the backswing shortens the left side of the body so it can pass between the spine and the ball and on the downswing assists the legs in driving the left arm back to the ball.

Swinging down, the body should never attempt to turn. After the weight has shifted to the left leg, the turn begins, but ther player will not feel as if he is turning. The upper body should feel still and well behind the hips as the hips slide. This brings the left arm down the correct track toward the ball. By doing this we will add the body-weights' power and the speed of the legs to the arm swing. After the shift is complete we will use the power of the lower right leg to turn the pelvis. The right leg runs around the posted left leg in a small circle. Done correctly the hips will turn very late in the action and very quickly.

Due to the design of the human body, one end of the spine or the other must move as the body steps from one foot to the other. Without spine movement we will lose our balance and the entire spine will move sideways. A person attempting to walk this way would look like a Frankenstein-type monster. To keep our swing-circle-center absolutely still, we must learn to maintain the exact tilt of our spines toward the ball throughout the swing. We can then use our leg and trunk movements to slide the lower end of the spine a substantial amount, left and right laterally, while maintaining this toward the ball tilt.

This lateral motion of the bottom end of the spine is vital, since it shifts the body weight from one foot to the other. This moves the bulk of the body's weight behind, then past the ball without moving the swing-circle-center. This way the body can actually run around in a circle while not moving the swing-circle-center. This adds speed to the arms just as the bowler runs to add speed to his throw. (Cont. on page 96)

In this photo series, on these two pages, since we are only dealing with the pivot we have eliminated the arm swing for clarity.

Jaacob is in the exact setup position he would be in to hit a full shot with any club. The tilt of the shoulders is caused by the tilt of the spine, notice that his spine is pointing at the left heel. (He would be tilted more toward the ball but the club representing the spine angle precludes this.) His spine is leaning away from the target due to the straight left leg and flexed right knee. The pelvis is tilted and paralell to the shoulders.

Shifting the weight now only requires pulling the right knee back to straight and flexing the left knee toward the ball. Doing these actions will cause the bottom end of the spine to slide right and the hips to turn a few degrees. The hips turn only that much and then they stop. The arrows show the movements of the knees and the slide to the right and turn of the hips. When you do this, you will then be in the position seen on the facing page.

Here Jaacob has executed the backswing weight shift. Note that the chest and hips are still in line wit`` each other. At this point, the shoulders turn behind the ball on the angle created by the tilted spine. The white line shows the pelvis is now tilted relative to the club (spine). This shows that the left side of the body has shortened and the right side has stretched. The powerful muscles on the back and front of the left side of the trunk have caused this and have stretched the opposing right side trunk muscles into position so they can work on the return.

You cannot attain this position unless the left knee flexes, the left heel slightly rises, the left ankle everts and the pelvis tilts. The photos and captions on the next two pages tell more about the very important ankle eversion.

Simply turning the shoulders from here will swing the arms and club back on the proper plane. The whole left side of the body can now pivot in toward the ball on the posted right leg, as the arrows show. Simply turning the left shoulder, once the weight has shifted, will turn the left side of the body between the spine and the ball.

The correct eversion of the left foot is very important in the Austin pivot. This is an example of how not to do it. By lifting and turning the left heel, intentionally or otherwise, the player loses the wind-up of the body. He also loses the power thrust upward of the left leg on the downswing, as well as the ability to time the body's actions with the feet. The slamming down of the slightly raised and everted left heel must happen at exactly the same time as the pick-up of the right heel to inhibit un-wanted early rotation of the hips. If the left heel works first, and thus out of sequence, the hips will turn instead of slide and this will cause an out-to-in hit of the ball. The arms will not return on the correct plane. This action is the classic over the top move which alters the correct club head path and robs power and accuracy.

Here the ankle has everted properly, this foot position frees up the hips to slide right as the spine tilts. The foot and ankle are pulled up and sideways by the muscles on the inside of the left upper leg as the left knee flexes in toward the ball. The weight on the foot is only the weight of the lower left leg and it rests on the inside edge of the ball of the left foot. The rest of the body weight that was on the left foot has transfered to the heel of the right foot, including the weight of the upper half of the left leg. Correctly done, the eversion sets the feet in perfect position to work together and time the action of the pivot. The left knee has slid under the chin and now gives balance to the turned body. The action will feel as if there is a wheel attached below the knee that rolls around under the knee and in front of the player. The balance will feel as solid as if we were a tripod.

(continued from page 91)

A good way to visualize the necessary movements of the legs and spine is to examine the natural motions we make when we walk. Because of the narrowness of his hips, a man walks in a manner that does not need much hip sway. His head moves slightly from side to side as he shifts from foot to foot. This motion is hard to detect since he is not putting one foot directly in front of the other but instead is walking on a very narrow track. If he were to move his feet on a wider track, say, shoulder width apart, head movement would be very apparent. On the other hand, when a woman walks, since her hips are generally wider than a man's, in her natural walk her hips move sideways. She is able to put one foot directly in front of the other and walk on a narrower path than a man without head movement. We might say she is moving beneath herself. This is the lateral hip movement without head motion that we seek. In the golf swing, men must educate the hips to move in the fashion that most women walk naturally.

Some teachers are advocating that the spine revolves in a manner similar to a rotating shaft driven through the head, down the spine and into the ground. Knowledgeable kinesiologists will tell you this concept is basically impossible to do without substantial head movement. Mike calls this move "wiping your butt on the grass" since the hips rotate instead of slide and the head sways - both these things diminish power and accuracy. Many of todays teachers also encourage head movement, we strongly disagree. In the Austin Golf Swing the swing-circle-center is the main fulcrum; it is the point that the arms, hands and club rotate around and it locates them for precise impact. Moving this fulcrum must be avoided since it is an extra unnecessary movement and limits the correct application of leverage. This pivot is the basis for the most powerful way to hit the ball. At the same time it is the only way we can swing without moving our heads. When we learn this pivot motion it will enable us to swing extremely hard at a ball that remains motionless.

Imagine that our mind's perception of the ball were a piece of film and that our eyes are a very slow shutter in our camera (head). If the camera were to move slightly, we would have a blurred, at best, photo. If it moved more we would have poorer and poorer picture quality, eventually having a very blurred image. Since the quality of this picture ultimately determines how pure our contact with the ball is, we can see how easy it would be to miss-hit it if we had blurry vision. Blurred, or shaky images tell us the head is moving.

HOW TO KILL THE BALL

Simply stated, we must pivot in a way that makes the ball a stationary target rather than a moving target. If the ball does not appear to be frozen in place as you swing, you have too much head movement. Our ability to accomplish this is one of the most vital parts of the perfect swing.

Precision contact combined with extreme power is solely controlled by our ability to pivot and get our weight behind the ball and then to reverse the motion and shift the weight ahead of the ball while maintaining this fixed swing-circle-center. Thus hitting the ball centered on the square club face.

For these things to happen in a powerful and precise manner each of the levers and hinges (joints) must function in accordance with their design. This is the realm of the science of kinesiology (the scientific analysis of the motions of the human body). Visualizing the motions of the body's muscles, levers and joints and understanding their actions will enable you to perform the proper movements necessary to strike the ball with a motion as perfect as is humanly possible.

The ability to create perfect shots is ultimately a product of the mind's ability to preconceive and visualize not only the flight of the ball but also the club face-ball alignment and the motions the body must do in order to produce that shot. It is this correct picture in our mind's eye that will direct our body in its motions exactly as the program moves a computer-controlled machine.

When you have mastered the pivot as taught in this book, you will find that your clubs will begin to show signs of wear in a dime sized shiny spot on the clubface. Gone will be the miss-hits, the topped, bladed or shanked shots and the power loss we get when we miss the sweet spot on the club.

By pivoting in this way we will be using the combined forces of our body's weight and the speed and power of our legs as we shift the weight of our body in the direction we want the swing energy to travel. At the same time, we will use the muscles of our legs to run around in a small circle, which rotates our pelvis in a similar manner. Together with the movements of the legs the muscles inside the trunk, that tilt the hips during the weight shift and pivot, send their energy up the rotating spine to the upper lever assembly, thus getting maximum power from our largest and most often misused power sources.

cont. on page100

Jaacob has executed a full turn. Because of the lateral shift of the hips he has been able to turn his whole body behind the ball without moving his head. The bow is ready to fire.

The only part of his body that is not behind the ball is the left leg from the knee down, and the only weight that is on his left foot is the weight of his left lower leg. 95% of his body weight is on the outside edge of his right heel. If he were swinging a club with his arms, the actions of the shoulder blades (you will learn later), would give him an additional 20 degrees of turn. He is fully coiled, and ready, to deliver the power of his legs and the inertia of his body weight to the shot. His shoulders and chest are turned 90 degrees while his hips have only turned about 45 degrees. As he swings down this hip-chest relationship must remain in tact until after the ball is gone. This keeps the legs driving and rotating the pelvis, which by rotating the spine, turns the chest.

Here Jaacob has executed the lateral hip slide by reversing the knee action. After the weight shifted, he turned his hips left by rotating the right heel out and driving the right hip down and around. If he were hitting a ball this body position would be at impact. The bow has released the arrow, the ball would be struck opposite the right hip, not in front of the body.

Jaacob's chest is still well behind the hips. He has kept the windup of the body and his right leg is in the process of running around the posted left leg. He is still in perfect balance and his swing-circle-center has not moved. His entire body has moved ahead of the ball with the exception of his head, right shoulder and lower right leg. If he were hitting a ball, those parts would also pass the white line after the ball was gone. If you compare this photo with the one on the facing page you will see how far he has moved his hips laterally. You should also note that the right side of the torso is very short and the left side is very long exactly the opposite of the previous position. His body has responded like a large bow, which shot the arrow targetward.

(continued from page 97)

We do this with a move we call posting up the legs. The right leg will become a vertical post for the body to rotate upon in the backswing and the left leg will do the same for the through swing. To accomplish this, the body must first shift the weight to the right foot and, then after the weight is shifted, turn the left shoulder behind the ball. Doing these moves, in this order, turns the left side of the body in toward the ball on the straight and posted right leg.

Since most of us have two legs of equal length, the head will remain at the same elevation because we will always have one leg straight. In accordance with this, our pivot will use straight legs to pivot on, we will pull the knee of the right leg back to straight, but not beyond, we don't want to quite lock the joint as we make our backswing. The right leg, now long, will serve as the rear post. Our left leg at exactly the same time shortens and lowers the hip as it flexes at the knee, hip and ankle. These actions, slide the hips laterally to the right and slightly to the rear. This transfers the weight to the now vertically posted right leg. Doing this keeps the head still. The slide of the hips to the right will momentarily actually go beyond the right hip. Then, when the shoulders turn, the hips will end up directly on top of the posted right leg.

The proper timing of the golf swing is created by the movements of the feet and knees. They must work together and at exactly the same time.

The downswing will be a reverse of this sequence as the hips slide laterally left caused by the action of stepping from the right foot to the left foot. This is followed by a turning through the shot by the right side of the body pivoting on the posted left leg in the forward swing. The above actions provide a powerful pivot and a stationary swing-circle-center; the double hinged gate will be working as designed.

The proper actions of the internal trunk muscles will be dealt with in the section on drills. For now just read along, the path is laid out for you and each movement you will learn must be supported by what you have previously learned.

Correctly done, the backswing stretches all of the muscles we need to power the downswing.

This stretching and releasing of energy, is very similar to the action of a bow and arrow. We pull the bowstring back, storing energy, and then let the bow release its stored energy into the arrow, thus producing its flight. An important thing to learn from this analogy is that if we do not pull the arrow straight back from the plane of the bow, we will get a very erratic flight. The same is true in the golf swing. We must make a backswing in the exact reverse of the downswing, and if we do, we can simply relax the arms, make our pivot, and let the return swing happen. Once we start the downswing pivot action, and start the club swinging, our only job is to watch the ball go. All of the effort of the golf swing is done two feet into the downswing.

The human body is well suited to making this motion as long as the lower end of the spine is allowed to move laterally. This is as if the spine were suspended by a sky hook from the swing-circle-center, rather than supported from below. In practice we must learn these specific motions which will allow the above action to occur as if the spine were suspended as described.

Naturally, it must be supported from below by the legs since that's how we are built.

The Austin pivot accomplishes the above objective with the additional benefit of putting the legs and hips in their most powerful position, with the body weight well behind the ball, while at the same time keeping the head in its original location. This pivot will also allow us to use the muscles in our legs and our torso in harmony and without causing undue strain so that we may enjoy many years of golfing pleasure. To those of you experiencing back pain you may find the correct pivot may strengthen your trunk muscles and thus relieve your suffering.

This statement is somewhat substansiated by the fact that I suffered severe back pain for many years due to a work related injury that the exercise of golf has helped and the injury does not bother my play anymore.

I do not claim that this pivot will be a miracle cure for any back pain you may now be experiencing. Also, I suggest that you consult with your doctor before beginning any new athletic activity. Simply stated, this movement conforms to the bodies design rather than violating it.

In review, the legs are the levers that provide the support and their actions are the main engine of the golf swing.

In this type of swing, the pivoting motion and the shifting of the weight must be done as separate motions that blend together into one. The correct weight shift and pivot is a compound motion and because the motion is compounded the energy produced is multiplied.

- A compound motion is one that uses multiple levers to increase power output. A couple of examples are locking pliers and a compound bow. Both of these examples produce much more force than the strength applied since the levers multiply the force. The body will fire its energy the way a bow fires the arrow.

- This lateral hip movement enables the golfer to get behind the ball as far as possible without moving the swing-circle-center.

- For the movement of the lower end of the spine to happen, the right knee must pull back and straighten and the left knee must flex and bend out toward the flight line. This knee action will cause the left hip and shoulder to lower, and by shortening the internal trunk muscles on the left side of the body, the left side of the pelvis will feel like it *rises.*

•   This feeling of the rising left side of the pelvis is caused by the contraction of the muscles within the left side of the trunk both on the back and front side of the torso. The lowest rib on the left side of the rib cage should feel as if it is touching the top of the left hip bone. To the observer the pelvis will appear to remain level, as the hips slide laterally.

- • On the other side of the body, the right hip will be lowered in relation to the ribcage and the space between the right hip and the lowest rib will be large.

As the body approaches the completion of this lateral hip slide to the right, the relaxing left knee which is bending (flexing) should be pulled to the right by the muscles on the inside of the upper left leg, thus putting the left leg in position under the chin to help maintain balance and help control head movement in the fore and aft plane. In order for this to happen the left ankle and foot must evert. Everting the ankle is rolling it over toward the body's centerline. The weight must come off the left heel. (See photos on the next 2 pages.)

The left shoulder will be pulled closer to the ground and the right shoulder will rise although both will still be square to the spine. This action will create the correct backswing arm plane without the need to raise the arms. More on this later.

After the weight shift is complete, the shoulders but not the hips, will turn to the right. When done correctly, the combined movements put the entire left side of the body (knee, hip and shoulder) between the spine and the ball. At the top of the backswing we will find our spine slightly tilting toward the target. It is very important that as we make this move we must also keep the original tilt of the spine toward the ball that we established at address.

The hips must double their movement to shift the body weight forward on top of the straightening left leg. If you were in the main room of a one room house and went out on the back porch and then went back through the house and out on the front porch, you would have traveled twice as far going forward as you did going back. Remember our hips move 6 to 8 inches to the right as we swing back, because of this they must move 12 to 16 inches left as we pivot down.

The drills you are about to learn will train your body to pivot perfectly. If you don't do them you will likely never perfect this motion.

CHAPTER 10

THE DRILLS

THE ROPE DRILL

These two pages describe the photo series on the next six pages in detail.

The first is the rope drill. This drill will increase the power of the swing and at the same time groove the feel for the legs and hips in the pivot. It will also teach you how to have a stationary head. This drill is the fastest and easiest way to feel the motions of the proper pivot. For the best results the use of a mirror is recommended. If you are lucky enough to have two mirrors at right angles to each other, so much the better.

If you have only one mirror do half of your exercises looking straight at it, and the other half with it over either your left or right shoulder. If you have two mirrors position them so that you can have both views at the same time.

We will need some props in order to get started with this drill: a ten foot length of soft rope (nylon clothesline is perfect) and something to loop the rope around that will sit on the ground and is fairly heavy, a golf bag will do nicely. Feed the rope through the loop where the handle attaches until you have two five-foot lengths one in each hand. A metal tent stake will also work well.

Take a stance by bending forward from the hips until your hands hang over your toes, wrap the rope around each hand and move forward maintaining the same tilt until the rope is taught and your arms are again hanging above your toes.

Begin walking in place, one knee forward as the other pulls bach to straight. Allow your heels to leave the ground and let your arms hang naturally. As you do this, begin to feel your weight shift from one foot to the other. Slide the hips to the right as the right leg straightens and to the left as the left leg straightens (this action is similar to the way females naturally walk, due to the width of their hips). Do nothing with your arms. Let them hang at your sides. Be sure to concentrate on pulling the knee, and not the hip back to straight. You are focusing on shifting the weight not turning.

- **Make no effort to turn, this drill is to train the body that the hips move left and right as the knees move fore and aft and as the heels rise and fall.**

While watching to see that your head does not move right or left, slide your hips laterally farther and farther each time until your hips are moving at least 6 inches to the right and left of where you started. The farther you shift the better.

If you are doing this correctly your belly button should be moving at least one foot since it is going six to ten inches each way while your head remains stationary. As this is happening, the shoulder should get higher on the side of the body that has the straight leg and lower on the side of the body that has the bent knee. To help this action, pull the lowest rib toward the crest of the hip bone as you go side to side. This will increase the distance that your hips move left to right and also the distance that your shoulders go up and down.

Remember, no part of your body is attempting to turn. The knees and feet are simply walking as the hips move laterally right and left and the shoulders go up and down. Now, as we continue the leg action of walking, bend forward 30 degrees from the hip sockets while keeping your spine and neck erect. Continue the walking and sliding laterally of the hips. You will be approximating the walk of a female chimpanzee impersonating Groucho Marx.

After doing the above drill for several minutes, add the actions of the arms and shoulders by pulling back one hand as the other hand is pulled forward by the rope. Do this so that the leg that is straight has the arm pulled back and the leg that is bent has the arm that is extended. Watch your head in the mirror and keep it still.

As you pull on the rope, feel your shoulders tilt and lower the upper arm bone as you retract the elbow of the pulling arm while extending the pulled arm. The elbow of the extending arm will then rise to the height of the hand.

Do this exercise every day for several minutes, and it will soon become second nature. Focus on the internal trunk muscles shortening the sides of the body. This drill perfects the pivot, it is the source of much power. We will need to learn it if we want to proceed.

We will modify this motion later as the golf swing evolves to increase power. For now just get the feel for the motion. On the following pages, you will find a photo sequence that will graphically illustrate this drill. Refer to it often as you re-read these pages.

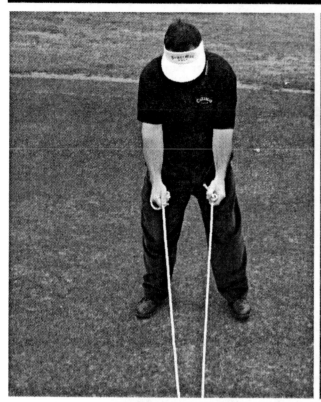
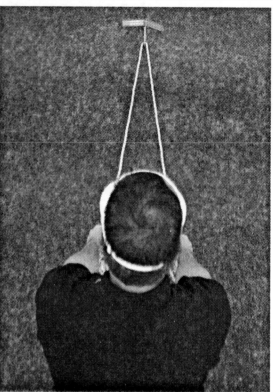

Here Mike Dunaway is ready to start the rope drill. He is in a centered stance with the weight distributed equaly on both feet and centered between the heels and toes. On the facing page the arrows show how the upper arm must rotate down from the shoulder so the elbow can pull straight back. This will begin to teach the arm trombone move you will learn later.

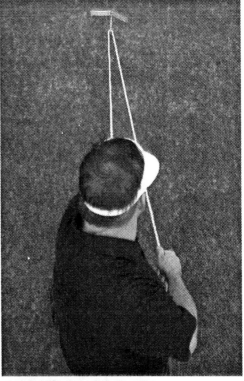

In this photo Mike is pulling on the rope with his right hand as his hips slide right, this causes the shoulders to turn on the proper plane and begins to give the player the feel for the proper arm action as well. As you can see, the weight has shifted onto the right foot and the head has not moved. The left knee should be directly beneath the chin thus providing a balance that will be as stable as a tripod. The right upper arm is lowering from the shoulder and the elbow is pulling in toward the hip. The pelvis has tilted and turned.

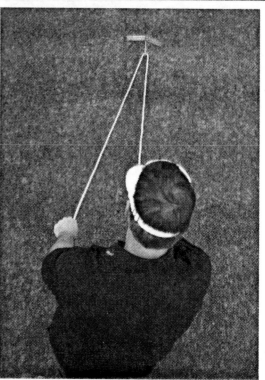

Here he is halfway through the drill and you can see how this drill moves the weight and causes the shoulders to turn on the perfect plane. The elbows and shoulders are also getting an education in the different way of operating that we call the "tromboning of the arms." If you keep practicing the Little Shot and do this drill for 5 minutes every day, you will improve your game in short order. The arrows show the elbow is rising as the arm extends. The right arm, as the elbow rises and the arm straightens, is sending power out to the releasing club head. Exactly the same way the extending arm throws a ball.

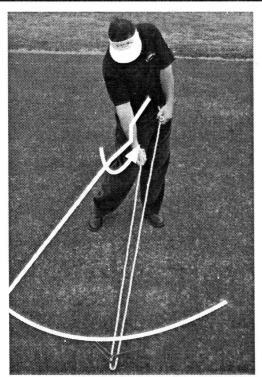

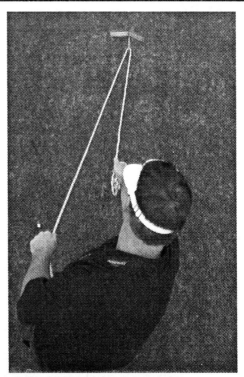

This drill is the basis for balance, combined with stability. The largest percentage of the power of the golf swing comes from these actions. Five minutes a day every day is your prescription. Take your medicine it will cure your ills. The white lines and arrows show how the club would be released as the hands make the crank action. This shows the conical release caused by the car crank hand moves graphicly. Since the pelvis has tilted the opposite way, the entire right side of the body can come through and hit the ball by rotating on the posted left leg.

The arrows show the movement that this drill trains the left upper arm to do, the elbow retracts as the upper arm swings down from the shoulder socket. This action is what keeps the hands on their correct plane both going back and releasing through. When this drill is done properly, the feel for the perfection of the Austin pivot and arm actions will program your mental computer. Five minutes a day every day is your prescription. Take your medicine it will cure your ills.

These photos are to show the same drill with a different body type, each player's angles will be naturally created based on the length of the arms, spine and legs. The arrows show the actions of the elbow as it retracts assisted by the downward and rearward action of the upper arm as it lowers from the shoulder socket.

Jaacob, who knows this method well, has produced the optimum body position for power and accuracy. If you compare this photo with the one of Mike Austin in the skeleton suit and Mike Dunaway on the cover at impact you will see that they are all nearly identical. These moves can be made by any body type, or size, since we all have the same bones and muscles. So, whether you are tall or short, fat or slim, do this drill.

THE POLE DRILL

The pole drill is to the turn what the rope drill is to the shift. Once you have somewhat mastered the shift get a broom stick or a ball retriever and work on this movement. Put a pole of roughly six feet in length behind your back and in the crooks of your elbows, take a stance about the same distance from the ball that you would be for a driver shot. Tilt forward about 30 degrees from the hips, this position is the basic starting position for all golf shots.

While focusing on the movements and the lateral slide of the hips we don't want to lose the weight shift as we learn this new move. The end of the pole will first go down as the spine tilts during the weight shift. As the weight shift ends, turn your shoulders. Correctly performed you will see that the pole points at the ball.

This drill is terrific for giving you the feeling for how low your left shoulder must go in order to turn the shoulders on the correct plane. It is also a super motion to train, strengthen and stretch the muscles of the trunk and lower spine that power the weight shift and turn.

This drill complements the rope drill and both should be practiced. First separatley and later, when swinging the club, the feels can be combined. It is very important to note that one of the things we are striving to attain as we do these drills is the rock-solid, stable head position that is the anchor of our swing-circle-center.

The better we can do these two drills, the better we will become at maintaining a perfectly still center to the rotation of the upper lever assembly of the arm, shoulder and club package.

This precision will give us solid, correctly struck shots just as a rifle held in a vice will deliver straighter shots than one that is fired while the shooter is riding a galloping horse. The photo on the facing pages shows that the initial movement of the pole is down as the weight shift begins, it then blends into a downward and rearward arc as the shoulders turn on plane. It deserves saying again, the first movement of the pole is down, then as it lowers the pole must be rotated and pointed at the ball.

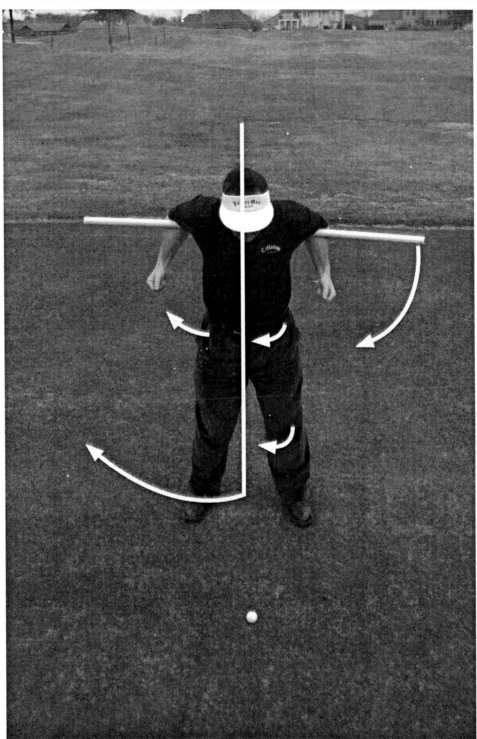

Here we have Mike Dunaway ready to demonstrate the pole drill. The picture was taken from a slightly elevated camera position to properly show the rotation of the pole. We used Mike in this photo series to show that the correct pivot can be done by any body type. Jaacob is twenty years younger than Mike and yet both do the pivot equally well.

Mike has made a full chest turn and has gotten all of his body, with the exception of his lower left leg, behind the ball. His weight is 95% on the center of his left heel and yet his head has not moved at all. It is still centered between his feet just as it was at address. The white line shows how far the lower end of the spine has moved laterally, while the upper end (and the swing-circle-center) remained fixed in space.

Here Mike has completed the shift and is almost to the point where the turn of the hips occur. At this point, the right heel must swing out toward the flight line to allow the knee to continue driving the hips. The club, if he had one in his hands, would be about two to three feet away from the ball and gaining tremendous velocity because of the dynamic weight shift and turn. Added to this power will be the speed of the rapidly catching-up club head. Boom! 350+ yard drives are common for Mike or Jaacob.

This is the same series of movements viewed from the side, it shows the way that the shaft revolves and the angle of the turning shoulders. Even though the bottom of the spine moves laterally a great deal, the tilt of the spine toward the ball must remain constant.

In this photo, we see just how well Mike has used his legs in the rope drill motion to shift his weight and turn his hips into position to allow him to point the shaft right at the ball. Notice that his shoulders are turning on a plane that is parallel to the shaft but slightly above it. The player will feel as if he has turned his left armpit to the ball. This turn and shift automatically creates the perfect backswing path and plane for the club head.

Mike has completed the weight shift by reversing the leg action he made going back. He has pulled the left knee back under the left hip. At exactly the same time he has lifted his right heel and flexed his right knee. This pair of actions combined with the lateral hip slide has returned the shaft around and down the correct plane. The turn of the hips is caused by the rotation of the right heel toward the flite line. The small arrow shows the direction of right heel travel, this action completes the hip turn, and allows the right leg to continue to drive the right hip. The rotating pelvis in turn rotates the drive shaft of the spine. This subtle yet powerful move will keep the left arm driving through the impact area adding power. The right heel at the finish will be directly above the toe. The path of the end of the pole will feel to be out toward right field; however, it will be traveling straight down the target line at the ball as the white circle shows.

This photo shows that the shift of the weight and the rope drill leg action will give you a perfectly consistant swing plane when it is used to control and power the shoulder turn. The path of the club will follow the rotation of the upper lever assembly. When we add the correct actions of the arms, we will totally control the swinging of the club head on a perfectly centered and controlled single plane around the swing-circle-center with minimal club face rotation around the shaft. We will accomplish all of this with no need to manipulate or control the club face as it returns since we will have never altered its alignment with the ball. The Austin Method approaches perfection as closely as is humanly possible.

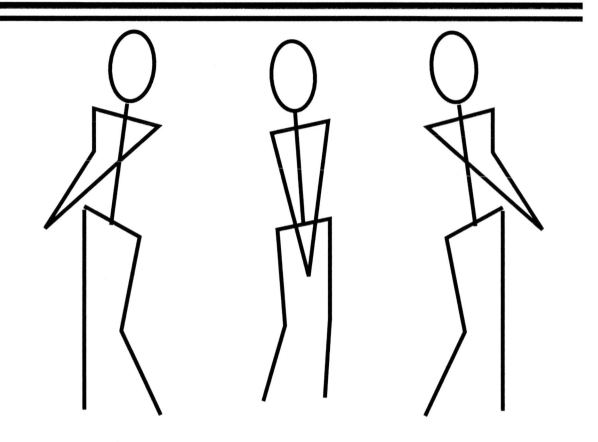

The sketches above show how the correctly done weight shift moves the "T" of the spine and the shoulders.

This movement tilts the shoulders and creates the proper stability of the swing circle center, and thus helps control the arc of the arms and hands while loading the swing with power.

THE KEYS TO THE PIVOT ARE THE ROPE AND POLE DRILLS. USE THEM; THEY OPEN MANY DOORS.

CHAPTER 11

THE SHOULDER BLADES

The golf swing that you are learning is an excellent physical workout. It will make you more flexible and is itself a wonderful way of gaining golf strength.

The best exercise for gaining strength and length in the golf swing is the golf swing itself. The more you practice these moves the stronger you will get. If you already work out with weights, use heavy weights and very few reps. This will build speed rather than endurance. Do very little work (bench press) on the upper chest area since large chest muscles restrict the left arm position across the chest. For old guys like your author, the focus should be on stretching and staying limber.

As stated earlier big muscles are not necessary. However, speed and supple quickness are and strength makes speed easier to attain. A solid, well-controlled Austin swing will give more distance with less effort than any other way of striking the ball.

THE SHOULDER BLADES

So far in this book, the focus of the motion has been on what the legs, feet and hips do to bring the body through the pivot. This section of the book deals with the actions of the levers attached to the top end of the human machine at the swing-circle-center. The arms will supply some power, but not with a hard physical effort. By returning to the position they occupied at address, the levers of the arms will add club head speed by the natural straightening action of the angles we flexed as we swung back. To this end, we will begin to discuss what the parts of the upper lever assembly do. And, how they do it.

The closest parts to the swing circle center are the shoulders, they form a see-saw type lever that uses the swing-circle-center as a fulcrum. Going back they are put into position by our shoulder turn. *Their motion is caused by the weight shift as the legs move the lower end of the spine and thus rocks and then turns the "T" formed by the spine and shoulders.*

The shoulder blades are not rigidly attached to the rib cage, but rather are sliding plates, with a ball socket, that holds the upper armbone. This allows the shoulder blades, and the shoulder sockets, to move closer, and farther, from the spine as the arms swing. We will use this action of the shoulder blades to gain additional turn without additional chest rotation.

When the shoulder blade moves away from the spine, the movement is called abduction, and when it moves closer to the spine adduction. It is not important to know these medical terms. It is important to know how these movements assist us in controlling and swinging the club. They locate the levers that transfer the power provided by the legs, to the rotating arm, hand and club lever assembly.

If you were to hold your chest from moving and turn your head to the right and left you would reach a point where the head cannot move any further. Any additional head movement will then cause the chest to turn. Most people can turn their heads about 80 to 85 degrees although some limber folks may attain 90 degrees or more.

Linda Blair not included.

(see photos next pages)

Since our head can only turn 80 or 85 degrees, or some fixed amount, any chest turn that exceeds our limit will move the head. We will want to stop the chest turn at that point in order to have a fixed center; however, by abducting the left shoulder blade and simultaneously adducting the right shoulder blade as we swing back we can gain 15 to 20 degrees of shoulder turn without moving the head.

In this photo, Jaacob is standing with his shoulders in a natural relaxed position. The shoulders are neither abducted nor adducted, they are in a neutral state.

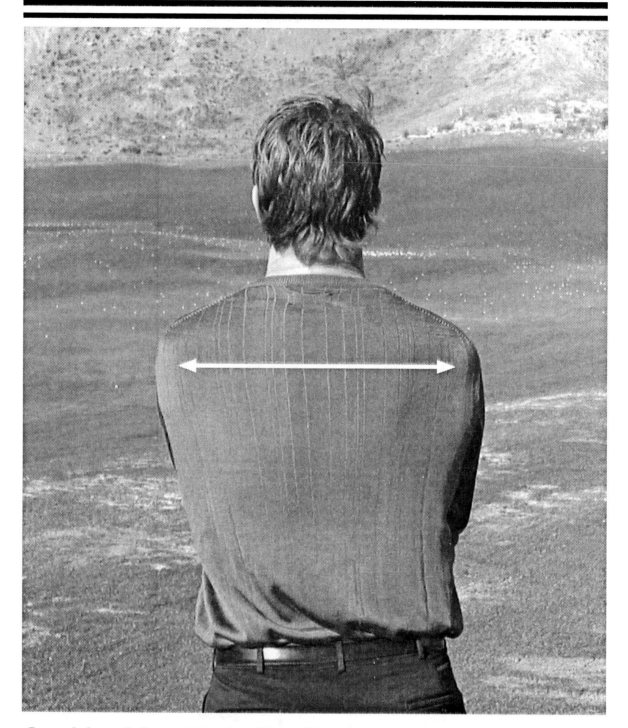

 Jaacob has abducted his shoulders. They have moved to the limits of their travel, each moving 3 to 4 inches around the curvature of the rib cage.

This has moved the shoulder sockets about 15 degrees around in front of the natural shoulder line.

In this photo Jaacob has pulled his shoulder blades closer to his spine. This action is called adducting the shoulders. At this point, his right shoulder is 15 or more degrees to the right of the natural shoulder line.

Here, we see Jaacob's shoulders in the position that they will be in at the top of the backswing. This picture is deceiving, he has not turned his chest, he has moved only the shoulder blades.

When we use the #7 position arm action, soon to be learned, it is the position that the left shoulder blade will be in until after impact. The right shoulder blade will return a small amount, but it too will still be slightly adducted at impact. Later as you make full swings, you will feel as if the whole swing happens behind you, due to the retarded chest and shoulder blades.

In this photo, Jaacob has turned his chest about where the average person can turn to without moving the head. As you can see, if he were to turn further than this his head would also turn. To gain an additional 20 degrees of shoulder turn he would next abduct his left shoulder and adduct his right shoulder. His left shoulder would end up at the end of the arrow greatly increasing his turn without moving his head. Of course, he would be tilted toward the ball, not standing erect. If we turned the shoulders this way, it would force the lift of the arms move that the Austin Method does not need, or want. Remember, the shoulders turn on the tilt of the spine.

CHAPTER 12

HOW THE BODY SWINGS THE ARMS

HOW THE BODY SWINGS THE ARMS

In the Austin Method the arms do not ever swing independently of the body. They go where the rotating spine takes them. Just as in a wheel, the turning axel causes the spokes to revolve with it. The arms never raise the club vertically, either by raising the club head vertically by lifting the thumbs, or by raising the arms from the shoulder sockets. This may sound crazy, because anyone with one good eye can see that the club is way up off the ground when it is behind the player's back. You will soon see how, in the Austin Swing, it gets there differently.

As we make our backswing the spine shifts and the weight moves laterally right. The bottom end of the "T" formed by the spine and the shoulders slides to the right. This causes the right shoulder to go up and the left shoulder to go down. The shift then blends into the turn. The tilted and now-turning "T" as it rotates, will swing the arms and club up without raising the arms, from the shoulder sockets, thus keeping the club on plane. (See Sketches of T page 122.)

To use the legs in the downswing we must keep the shoulders and chest wound as far behind the hips as they are at the top of the backswing. If we don't, the back muscles will be doing the work and they are not capable of rotating the lever assembly as powerfully or as accurately. Losing the wind-up will cause the loss of the drive of the legs. Just as one car towing another can not pull if the rope is slack. When the coil is maintained the left arm will travel around the swing-circle-center exactly as a spoke goes around with the axel, and at the same speed as the axel. In Austin's words, "If the spokes do not travel with the axel the wheel breaks down." We also disconnect from the power source.

Since we did not raise the arms on the way back we will not have to lower them as we swing back down. The shift forward from the right leg to the left leg creates the correct downswing plane, and club head path, automatically as long as we keep the body wound up by keeping the chest turned right of the hips.

The hips slide laterally left, and the left knee straightens, driving the left shoulder up. As this happens the right leg runs around the posted left leg, driving the pelvis in a circle, which also rotates the spine. The spine then turns the chest, thus returning the left arm back down the perfect path. When we do this the left arm is being driven by legs as they turn the chest through the shot.

In our mechanically perfect golf swing, we have found how the power of the legs and the shifting of the weight send the power up the spine.

As we make the back swing, what we will be doing is best described as raising the left arm sideways. To feel this, stand up straight and then tilt forward about 30 degrees. You would now be roughly at the address angle, your left arm should be angled out slightly and hanging over your toes. You will be in the posture that you see in photo #1 on the following pages.

From this position, grasp your left wrist with your right hand and, keeping the left arm extended, pull your left arm to your right and sideways across your chest, toward your right shoulder. You will find yourself in the position shown in photo #2 with your left hand about one forearms length to the right of the right hip. We call this the #7 position since the shoulders and left arm form a number 7 when viewed from in front of the players chest.

BELIEVE IT OR NOT, THIS POSITION IS AS HIGH AS THE LEFT ARM WILL FEEL TO TRAVEL RELATIVE TO THE SPINE AND CHEST.

If you now executed the body tilt and turn to the right that you have been practicing, with the rope and pole drills, you would find yourself in the perfect top-of-the backswing position (photo #3). Your shoulders should be 45 degrees to the right of your hips and your back should be turned to your imaginary target.

Now, do not move anything above the waist (including the waist) and using the lateral hip slide and the rope drill leg action, slowly rotate back down to address by leading your left elbow with your right knee. It is crucial to slide the hips laterally left. This lateral slide re-tilts the spine for the forward rotation. You should now be in the position of photo #4. If you were in the act of hitting the ball, this is impact position lacking only the swinging club. The left arm should still be in the same location, relative to the chest, as it was at the top of the backswing. Your belly button should be pointing left of the flight line and your chest should be parallel, or slightly open to the flight line.

You have just made the most powerful move in golf, the perfect pivot, combined with the maintenance of the body coil all of the way back down and through the hit of the ball. The left arm has been powered by the legs and the shift of the body's weight. On the next pages we will see a drill for this action.

Photo # 1

From this position, we will do the drill.

From the address position, grasp your left wrist with your right hand, pull your left arm directly at your right shoulder. Keep it pressed to the side of your chest and clamped to the top of the pectoral (breast) muscle. The right arm must bend at the wrist, elbow and shoulder joints for this to happen. (see facing page)

The photo below shows the position you will attain. As the turn begins, the tilt of the spine and the turn of the shoulders will rotate the left arm to the perfect top-of-the-backswing slot, as you will see in the following photos.

Photo # 2

This position is the limit of travel for the left arm. At first it will feel quite low to you and you will feel as if your backswing is very short. This is the amount of travel the left arm makes relative to the body. The left arm and shoulder now form a # "7"

The left arm will get higher, due to the weight shift that tilts the shoulders, and the turn of the chest combined with the actions of the shoulder blades. However, the swing will feel to be more around the hips rather than the shoulders.

The body has taken the arm back. The weight shift is complete and so is the turn. The left side of the body has shortened and the right side has lengthened. The left arm feels to be in the same low position that it was in the last photo #2. Once the weight shift and chest turn have been completed and the shoulder blades have reached the end of their travel, the bow string is fully stretched.

If we were swinging a club, the right shoulder blade would have taken the left hand closer to the target but not any higher. The left arm has now attained the #7 position and will remain in this position until after the ball is struck. For this to happen the chest must not unwind from the hips. The legs and feet must shift the weight and rotate the left arm back down. The foot and leg actions combined with the internal muscles that shorten the sides of the body return the left arm down the perfect plane into the ball. The left arm has never gotten higher than the right shoulder and the combined actions have placed the left arm in the ideal plane for the return weight shift and pivot to bring the arms, hands and club to the ball thus eliminating the over-the-top move.

Here we see how the return slide of the hips, and the turn of the right knee and ankle, brings the left arm down the perfect path and powers the shot all of the way from the top of the backswing through impact with the left arm still supported by the chest and driven by the mass of the body. The legs have done the work and the chest has remained turned to the right of the hips. The legs have powered the return of the left arm.

Due to this move, we will make contact with the ball opposite our right hip rather than in front of the body, so long as we keep the legs and hips leading the upper body. The right heel must rise to start the downswing and the right knee must attempt to stay ahead of the left elbow. This is the return position of the drill. For maximum power the right knee should attempt to stay in front of the left elbow as the photo shows.

It is the maintenance of the chest staying back feeling that causes the power of the weight shift and legs to do the work, rather than giving the job to the unwinding of the back muscles. Unwinding will not produce as much power and, sooner or later, will cause us back pain or worse. At impact, the left arm should still be in the same location relative to the chest as it was at the top of the backswing, your belly button should be pointing 45 degrees left of the flight line and your chest should be parallel to the flight line. If you were hitting the ball, you would not be hitting the ball in front of your belly, you would be hitting the ball alongside your right hip.

Wait a minute, you're not done. The right calf muscle, and right knee will continue to drive the buttocks down, around and forward thus driving the left arm another 45 or so degrees beyond where the ball was. (see photo #5). This is where the throwing action of the right arm (which you'll learn next) and the free-swinging club head's energy will pull the left arm off the chest, after impact, as the right arm swings across the front of the body into the reverse #7 position.

The actions of the arms as they swing beyond the ball are the exact mirror images of what happened on the way back in the backswing. The right-handed man's finish is the left-handed man's backswing except for the hand locations on the grip.

This is the power move in our golf swing. The perfect pivot returning the left arm using the drive of the legs combined with the target-ward movement of the weight of the body.

When we keep the shoulders and chest turned as far as possible to the right of the hips we maintain the body coil all of the way back down and through the hit of the ball. An action hinted at by Jim Mc Lean's concept of The 'X' factor.

Returning the left arm perfectly back down the proper plane was done by the actions of the feet and knees combined with the contracting of the stretched torso muscles. Due to these moves the body's largest and most powerful muscles were driving and controlling the path of the left arm. Later we will combine this powerful pivot with the arm actions after they are both totally understood.

In this photo, Jaacob has stayed down until the right arm is pointing at the target. Here the right arm is in the reverse of the #7 position.This is where the right arm would go if we were throwing something target-ward while rotating on a tilt. The lines show how far ahead of the arm the club shaft is, showing the fullness of the wrist release. Not visible in this photo is the left elbow which is folding (tromboning) and getting out of the way.

The above actions are accompanied by the swinging of the club with the right arm and the release of the swinging pendulum of the club.

 The learning of the arm movements come next, and we will call these actions the motions of the cranked lever assembly. The way we do these actions and use the arms as cranked levers is through the coordinated movements of the wrists, elbows and upper arm bones in an action we call tromboning the arms.

The concept we will be using also requires us to have a different understanding of the swing plane. I call this the concept of the rotating plane. As little as I like to have to speak about more than one action at a time, these two things are intertwined so it is unavoidable.

CHAPTER 13

THE ROTATING PLANE

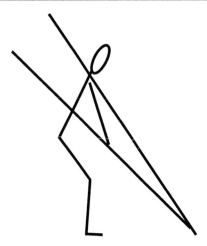

This sketch shows the plane created by the lie angle of the club, we call this plane the shaft plane. The plane that sits on the players shoulders is the Hogan plane. In the commonly taught golf swing the plane is said to steepen in the area along the arm line and rise to the upper plane. This is the classic "lift it up and then bring it back down" action necessary when we attempt to swing on this type plane.

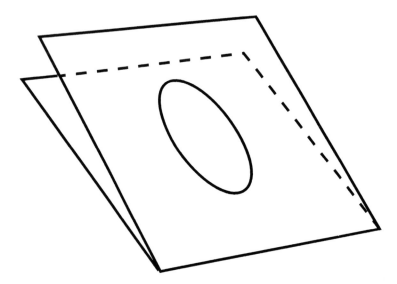

The changing of the plane's movement can be eliminated through the move we call the tromboning of the elbows and the non-lift of the thumbs or the arms from the shoulder sockets. In the Austin Method the club head is always on the top plane while the hands are always on the lower plane. The difference in height, we see of the club head, is caused by the arm shaft angle which keeps the hands beneath the shaft. Thus, the club head is above the hands at the top of the backswing. This is not visible when the backswing is complete due to the fullness of the turn.

HOW TO KILL THE BALL

THE ROTATING PLANE

The common concept of the golf swing has the club swinging on a flat circle that could be described as an imaginary sheet of glass or plastic. This concept has the club traveling endwise toward the ball and then, as the club approaches the ball, the arm-shaft angle (which has cocked up) opens and the arms turn over in the area where the ball is. After that complex action the hands follow the club head through to the finish.

When a player attempts to swing with this concept in mind, the club head travels straight away from the ball and up as the right hand gets under the shaft causing the plane shift. The club head is then followed up its arc by the hands that now are (in the Austin Method) in the wrong arc.

When we swing this way, the body (axle) which is turning right is actually going in a different direction from the spokes (arms and club) which are now rising from the shoulder sockets and rotating the club face to conform with this change of swing plane.

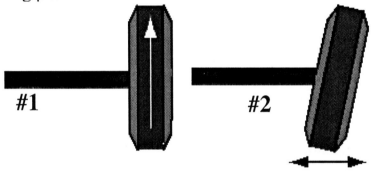

Sketch #1 above left shows a wheel that is traveling in the same direction as its axle it is turning smoothly. The wheel on the right (sketch #2) is not traveling in the same direction as its axle, the result is a wobbling wheel. This action dissipates power and control, just as it would in your car.

In the commonly used plane concept, the plane is said to shift as the club gets on top of the right hand and then to drop back down as the club comes back into the ball. Many excellent players swing this way, but the motion has a lot of moving parts that must be coordinated. Thus, they have days when it's easy and days when it's not. The Austin Method keeps the club head on one constant plane. That one single factor, among many, makes the Austin Method create a swing that is more reliable.

When we try to swing the club onto this kind of plane the arms have to rise from the shoulders and they get very high at the top of the backswing. This is the position that many good golfers are attempting to attain, as can be seen in photographs of some of our top players. This is not the position that we want to swing to at the top of the swing (granted the common swing with high arms looks pretty), but when we swing the arms back and up like this we create many problems and potential errors for ourselves in the downswing.

As we have stated earlier, the club head is then coming at the ball hosel first, with the face wide open, and it must be manipulated back to square. The player also has to get the club back on the original plane. Those of us who use the Austin Method will not have either of those problems to deal with since we do not change planes or open and close the blade. Ask any frequent flyer and he will tell you, when you have to change planes, you can easily miss your flight.

Instead, we will have the easier problem of (one) learning to use the weight shift and pivot to control the rotating plane through the movements of our spine as it shifts back and forth, combined with (two) the proper use of the arms to not lift the club off the plane as the elbows fold, and (three) using the forearm windup and the free release of the hands to swing and control the club face.

Since everything we need to conciously do occurs in the backswing (the free release of the hands is not controlled) our learning will be easier. The golf swing is not easy to learn using either of the two stated methods and there will be those who have grooved their actions and are able to hit excellent shots who will disagree with what we do. We do not say that their method is inferior, just more complex. Only time will prove which method becomes the standard.

Over the next pages we will show through photos, sketches and captions the rotating plane and the cranked levers of the tromboning arm action. Study the graphics and the captions carefully and you will soon understand the actions of the lever assembly. Only when we grasp the concept of the rotating plane and how it relates to the cranked lever assembly and the counter-rotating shaft can we see the simple elegance of the Austin Method. Those who learn it can become champions, and many already have. We who use it believe it to be the concept of the future; although it is strange that it comes to us from a voice from the past.

THE PLANE OF THE SWING TURNS WITH THE CHEST

The concept of the flat plane was the work of the great Ben Hogan. His theories advanced the game considerably and, as you can see in his book, his hands never went above shoulder height. Anyone who examines Ben Hogan's swing photos will see that his arms never went up. Thus he was always described as being a flat swinger. Hogan also hooked the ball early in his career and later compensated for the bounce pass, roll over arm movements, by weakening his grip and holding a bowed left wrist through impact.

Mr. Hogan used a different hand release than Mr. Austin, but because of his similar flatter swing plane his spokes were traveling more with his axle and he was renowned as being a very consistent ball striker. Today, the bulk of instructors have the concept of the entire shaft of the club swinging on Hogan's plane with the rolling arm action. In the Austin Swing the club head, not the shaft, does swing on Hogans flat plane of glass around the body but the plane does not shift or tilt. Due to the counter rotation of the forearms, the free release of the wrists can be used without the potential for the unwanted hook.This is a radically different concept and can only be understood through pictures and captions.

However, there are some words that can begin to set the stage for our learning. Imagine a wrecked car lying at about the tilt angle that the arms would swing around as they orbit our body. If the front tire were spinning slowly we could see the valve stem come around and we could see that as being the point of the arm shoulder triangle from whence the club swings. If someone sitting inside the car were to turn the steering wheel to the right, as the tire rotated right, we would get a pretty good approximation of what actually happens in the back swing. The hands (valve stem) would go slowly around and up as the tire itself turned right, assuming that the tire rotated at the same speed that the steering wheel did. (See sketches following page).

As the tire rotated to the top, the valve stem would stop at the top. If the tire then reversed directions, and as it did if the steering wheel also turned left, it would rotate the tire so that when the valve stem returned to the down position it would be in line with the direction that the car would be traveling (if it hadn't wrecked). The hands and club (valve stem) are returned square to the flight line by the rotating body through the release area. After impact the steering wheel (arc of the hands) keeps turning left and the valve stem ends up back on top.

This page illustrates that the body is rotating out from under the flat plane that Mr. Hogan envisioned both on the backswing and on the follow-through. This is the concept of the rotating plane and it will help you to see, in your mind's eye, the movements that the body must do to cause the club to swing around the axel of the spine and at the same time control the clubface.

In this sketch of a car wheel I have added a triangle that represents the shoulders and the arms. See it as a "T" shirt with a bulls eye logo. The wheel turns to the right exactly as the front wheel of your car would. The bottom of the wheel would stay in the same spot as in the sketches below. The sketches on this page show the wheel with the rotation caused by the shoulder turn. On the following pages you will see what the arms do to allow the club head to swing.

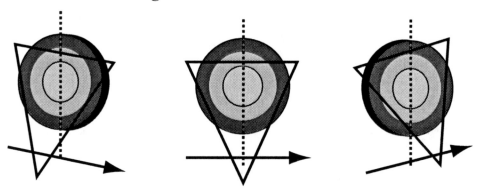

These sketches show what happens when the chest turns. The arms, which are controlled by the shoulders, turn with the chest.

The club head also swings inside the flight line as it follows the rotating chest and will correctly follow the Hogan plane only if we counter rotate the forearms and swing the club shaft in a cone. In the Austin Method if we raised our arms to accomplish this we have made an error.

Since the human body can only swing the club from one side of the body to the other, we can only swing the club where the chest is pointing. If a player were to sit against a post that is less than the width of his back while seated on a stool and swing the club only with his arms he could easily see an arc that was the same on both sides of the ball. Doing this would swing the club on a plane that is relative to the chest. If he were to turn the stool 90 degrees so that his back were now to the target and swung the club with the same arm movements, he would be swinging the club on the same plane relative to the chest and the axle of the spine, but the plane would have rotated 90 degrees away from the ball and he could not even hit it.

This is what happens in the golf swing as soon as you turn your chest away from the flight line. The plane of the swing rotates with it. Attempting to swing the club onto the plane that your body has just turned away from requires many complications to an otherwise simple action. The arms will have to rise and the club will not follow the axle of the spine. The wheel will wobble.

In the Austin Method, the triangle of the arms and shoulders will turn the club inside the flight line and it will follow the natural arc caused by the turn of the chest. The club head will swing up the Hogan plane not caused by the raising of the arms and thumbs but instead because of the spine tilt we set at address, and the tilt laterally caused by the hip slide as we shifted our weight, combined with the conical action of the club-head.

The chapter on arm movements explains this action thoroughly. The trombone action of the arms will keep the hands from rising above the plane we set them in at address. The return action will simply be a reverse of what we did going back and it will feel easy and powerful. The whole lever system of the body and arm assembly, by simply reversing, will return the club head square and centered. This will only happen if you pivot well and allow the forearm muscles to relax and unwind. By making the backswing the exact reverse of the downswing we stretch all of the muscles we will be using in the hit. The stretched muscles will return the club perfectly and without the need of concious control. This method is the mechanically and anatomically correct way to swing the golf club. Because of that, it will provide power and accuracy and, since it does not violate the design of the body, will provide the player with a long playing career. Mike Austin could still hit the ball over 300 yards until his stroke at age 79.

The Swing-Circle-Center is the main fulcrum of the golf swing.

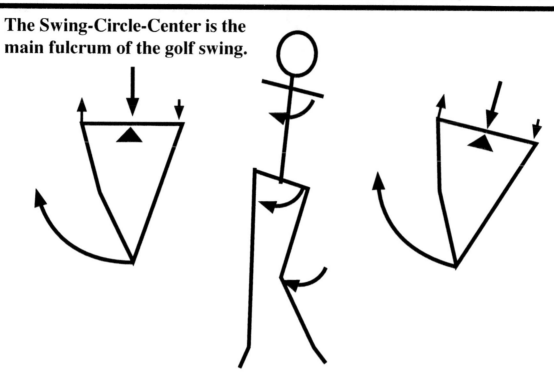

The weight shift moves the hips laterally. After the weight shift is complete the pelvis rotates on top of the straight right leg. This action causes the rib cage to turn which brings the arms and shoulders onto the perfect rotating plane.

Here is a T-shirt with the tire on it. It is impossible for the player to turn his chest to the right or left and not have the tire turn with it. This concept should change the way you think of the swing. We do not try to swing the club head back and up while relating it to the flight line. The club head must swing inside the flight line to conform with the rotating chest. As Mr. Austin says, "There are no straight lines in the golf swing. The club swings in an arc on the oblique plane, which rotates. The only straight line in a circle is its radius." When the correct counter rotation of the forearms is applied, the club head will appear to go straight back and up to the player. To an outside observer the club head will rotate on a perfectly tilted circle, as the club swings on the oblique plane.

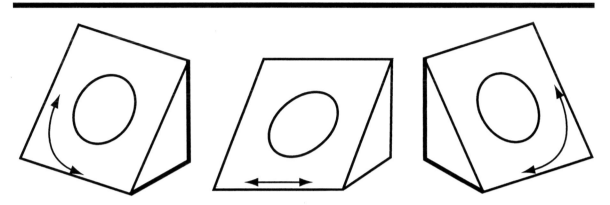

These 3 sketches speak volumes. As can be plainly seen, the circle of the hands within the plane must turn with the chest to swing the club on the inclined plane. These blocks which show phases of the swing are positioned next to each other for visual clarity, in the golf swing the circle merely rotates with the chest.

As the arrows show, the club is always being swung relative to the chest. The rotating chest returns the club through the ball due to the pivot. Because of this, the actions of the legs, and internal trunk muscles, control and power the club's return on the correct plane and path. For this reason the downswing path of the left arm must be felt to swing across the line from inside out as we swing down. This direction is caused by the lateral slide of the hips as the weight shifts. Then as the weight shift ends, and the body turns left, the actual path of the club head is straight down the line. After impact, because the body continues to turn, the club swings back up around and in.

People who are inherent slicers of the ball often do so because of this factor. When you attempt to hit the ball straight down the line, due to the rotation of the body turning the plane, it causes the club head to cross the flight line from out to in even though your view and your feel will be that you swung straight down the line. This is a common problem, and the best way to tell if it's your problem is to look at your divots. If they point left of where you were aiming you did not allow for the rotating plane factor. In the Austin Method this is caused by a mis-timing of the actions of the knees and heels. The right heel must come up exactly as the left heel goes down and the hips slide left. If they do not work exactly together the body will turn too soon. Properly done, if you use the Austin Pivot and release, your divots will be perfectly straight and will have square ends, they will be the size and shape of dollar bills.

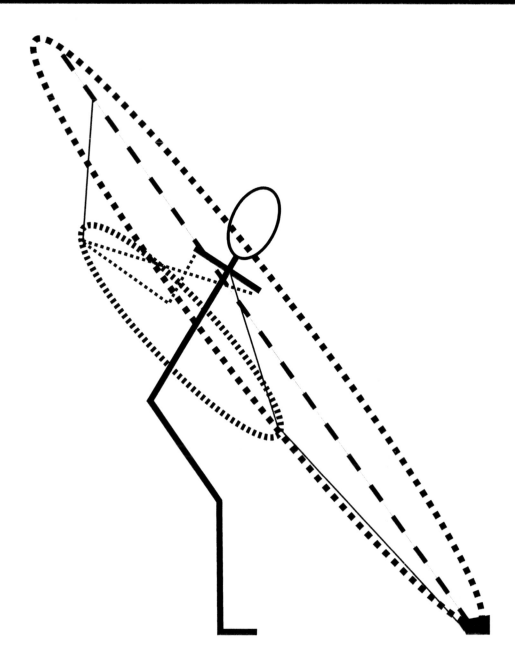

This sketch is rather busy, but if you look closely, you will see that the small dotted circle is the arc of the hands. The large dotted circle is the arc of the club head. Look closely and you will see that they are nearly parallel, one above the other; this is because we never raise the club head by raising the thumbs or the arms from the shoulder sockets. In the Austin Method the club head plane is controlled by the pivot and the conical action of the club caused by the counter rotation of the club head we learned and practiced in the Little Shot.

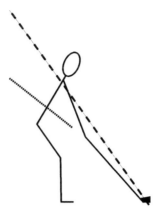

In this sketch our player is in his stance. It is plain to see that the hands are below the club head plane and are in position to turn on a plane more around the hips than around the shoulders.

The club head, however, is in position to swing around the shoulders since the arm-shaft angle does not change. Due to the shift of weight and the resultant tilt of the spine, the clubhead will swing around on Hogan's plane perfectly, provided that we don't lift the arms from the shoulders or raise the club by lifting the thumbs and thus change the arm-shaft angle we set at address.

In the sketch above, we see a circle representing where the hands would go if we could swing without bending the elbows. The small arc shows just how little the club swings from the wrists. 45 degrees each side of the center.When we combine the wrist arc with the elbow and shoulder action, we will get the full swinging action of the club, 90 degrees each side of center. Remember the plane of the club head is always above the hands even though it won't look that way at the top of the backswing when the club shaft is pointing down the line.

PHOTO SERIES

On the next pages you will see several photos and captions that will visually show the concept of the rotating plane.

In the photo above Jaacob is in the address position except for his hands which need to be spread to hold the hoop. As the series unfolds watch how his body action swings the arms around the path and you will see why he has length. Also, watch his hands and they will show you why he has accuracy.

Here Jaacob has shifted and began his turn to show that the plane does not rotate unless the chest rotates and since we all turn our chests (hopefully) this shows why we cannot swing on one flat plane. The arms are taken inside by the turn and so is the club, however, the conical action of the counter rotating forearms raises the clubhead to the correct plane. The white line shows the rotation of the plane, the arms can only swing the club in the direction of the arrows. The arrow is now 45 degrees to the flight line.

HOW TO KILL THE BALL

Here we see the same body position as the previous photo (lower left) except in this shot he has turned his shoulders as he would in a normal backswing, the rotating plane is easy to see. Since the plane has rotated, if the arms swung the club without the chest turning back to the ball the player could not even hit the ball.

The plane has rotated with the turning chest in the shot below. From this position the arms swing the club in the direction (arrow) that the hoop is pointing.

The club head would be swung away and behind Jaacob in the direction of the arrow so that as it came around the circle it would feel to be swinging out to right field. The natural return of the rotating plane will square itself to the flight line as the pivot of the body rotates the plane back around. The next photos will show how this happens.

In this photo the drive of the legs as the weight shifts laterally is evident.

The left shoulder has been driven up by the straightening left leg, the right heel has lifted and is about to turn out, and the right knee is trying to stay ahead of the left elbow. The right side of the body has shortened, it can now pass between the spine and the ball. The photo above and the photo below were taken at the same time.

From this view it is plain to see how far behind the lower body the upper body remains, the legs and body weight have done their work. The return weight shift has been completed and the right leg will now drive the pelvis and the chest rotating the plane back to square.

This is the position we want to attain at impact. The right arm is in the process of straightening and the right elbow is coming up to the height of the left elbow.

The left leg is straight and in position to act as a post so that the body weight can rotate on it as the right leg runs around it. Again the photo below was taken at the same time. Notice throughout this series that the hands never would have had the club face out of line with the arc of the swing. Accuracy is assured. The rotating plane has returned to square.

The only thing being muscularly moved through this area of the swing is the right heel which is turning out and the right leg which is driving the right buttock down around and forward. The turning chest has brought the arms around so that they can swing the club down the flight line. The hands and arms are freewheeling and responding to the weighted club head. The laws of nature, gravity and centrifugal force, are in control.

If you were going to toss someone a bag of balls, would you toss it like this? This action is what Hogan taught as a basketball bounce pass action. I don't think so. If you did it would be very hard to catch and, if the bag were open, the balls would fly wildly. Yet this hand motion is used by almost every golfer in the world and, unless perfectly timed, they wonder why their shots are inaccurate. As they swing back, the right hand goes below the left hand opening the blade. Look at the position of the left hand on the throw. This is the classic supination move that has been in style for years. This move is necessary to return from the backswing actions. On the next page, you will see some different hand actions. I think you will agree that they are more likely to be accurate.

Here, Mike is tossing the bag by pivoting, and by rolling it, the bag would simply go straight back and around. This is the basis for our body and arm movements. As you will see, as we go on, this is mechanically simpler. Ask any mechanic; a well made simple machine is very reliable and easy to repair if things go wrong. Doing this motion also forces good body action.

Since, due to gravity, the hand action occurs naturally at the bottom of the release this body action greatly simplifies the swing. Look at how the right arm can throw the bag. In the golf swing the right hand releases the same way. The forearm muscles that move the hand in this fashion are very strong in this direction.

CHAPTER 14

AS THE BODY SWINGS THE ARMS, THE HANDS SWING THE CLUB

USING THE ARMS AS CRANKED LEVERS VERSUS THE WRIST ROLL

As you know by this time, the way the golf swing has been taught for many years, the wrists have been used in a vertical motion combined with a rolling-over action as the club face is first rolled open in the backswing and then rolled closed as the club is hitting the ball. In this action the right hand crosses over the left.

This is necessary since, as the swing is commonly taught, the club face has been rolled open 90 degrees. These moves necessitate the return roll of the arms in order to turn the face of the club toward the ball and target as the club approaches the ball so as to not hit the ball with the hosel of the club. When we swing the club this way, this rolling of the face around the shaft reduces the accuracy of the shot and reduces the power that can be transmitted into the ball, it does not make full use of the available leverage.

Due to the elbow and upper arm motions we will use the club face remains square to the points on the compass as it travels around our bodies. As a bonus, the club will automatically swing into the perfect slot at the top of the swing. Once we learn and practice these movements we will swing the club on plane every time and it will feel easy.

Keep doing the rope and pole drills, as well as the Little Shot, and we will soon combine them.

Due to the different way that we use our arms and wrist action, the club head will swing on Ben Hogan's type of plane throughout the entire swing. As this happens the club face will maintain its alignment with the ball.

The club head itself always stays above the hands at the arm-shaft angle we established at address. We use the elbows to allow the sides of the arm-shoulder triangle to shorten, thus gaining a large amount of club head travel.

This motion, combined with the free hinges of the releasing wrists, will cause the club head and club face to travel in a precisely controlled conical arc. The actions of our hands and elbows are much like the actions we would use to crank-start an old fashioned car or jack up a car with a scissors jack.

This photo begins to show how the arms are used as cranked levers. The lowering of the upper arm bone from the right shoulder socket has allowed the right elbow to retract and trombone in toward the right hip. The point of the shoulder-arm triangle at the hands is now directly in front of the right shoulder. The right side of the triangle has shortened. The right elbow is beginning to move away sideways, as if opening the arm pit, giving us more right-hand wrist-cock but not more left-hand wrist-cock. As you can see, the left wrist is slightly bowed and the right wrist is fully cocked. The thumbs have not raised and are level with the forearms. The club has cocked sideways rather than up. From here a powerful hit could be made by simply shifting the weight to the left foot and hitting through with the right hand. For a complete release the club and arms must mirror this position, after the hit, on the opposite side of the body.

The upper bone of the right arm at this point rotates in the direction of the curved arrow from within the shoulder socket as the right shoulder blade adducts (slides toward the spine). This action raises the left arm, not up, but sideways across the chest (in the direction of the arrow on the shaft) as the left shoulder blade abducts (slides away from the spine). This motion allows the right hand and right upper arm bone to swing out and around the right elbow (curved arrow), thus swinging the left arm directly toward the right shoulder. Instead of raising the hand plane, the lowering and retracting action of the right arm allows the right forearm, as it winds up, to get above the right elbow without rising This action keeps the clubface on plane and much simplifies hitting.

Returning through the hitting area we simply relax our arms and the wound up forearms return the club head perfectly, simply by unwinding. An additional benefit is that as we swing through the left elbow gets out of the way thus eliminating the blocked shot. It is this relaxation through the hit that allows the club head's weight to swing the club, hands and wrists through the shot as freely as a swinging pendulum. The photo opposite shows an additional action caused by the folding of the elbows. This action of the elbow gives the club 45 additional degrees of travel relative to the left arm while still keeping the club face perfectly aligned with the ball. Because of the unique way we use our elbow we end up with 90 degrees of club-arm angle without raising the thumbs.

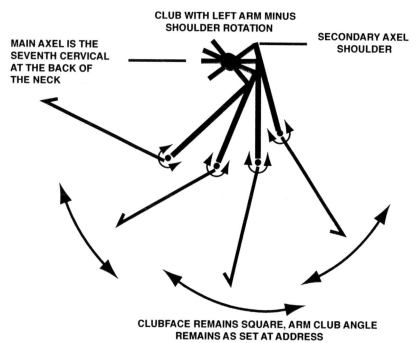

CLUB WITH LEFT ARM MINUS
SHOULDER ROTATION

MAIN AXEL IS THE
SEVENTH CERVICAL
AT THE BACK OF
THE NECK

SECONDARY AXEL
SHOULDER

CLUBFACE REMAINS SQUARE, ARM CLUB ANGLE
REMAINS AS SET AT ADDRESS

This sketch shows how the club head releases around the wrist axle in the full swing. In the Austin method the club face always stays in the same place relative to the shaft. Since we are not rolling the shaft open and closed, the club head remains on the same side of the shaft. Players who use the roll-the-club-face open, and then roll-it-closed swing, so commonly taught and regarded as perfect, will say your club face is shut at the top of your swing.

We who know that it is not shut, merely rotated without opening, will know that we are doing this swing right when we hear that. Be sure to thank them for the advice.

This photo shows the elbows ability to shorten the right arm and attain the normal 90 degrees of wrist-cock. This photo is of a short pitch shot and it shows that the club shaft gets parallel to the ground as well as parallel to the shoulders.

In any shot longer than a short pitch shot we would not attain this position for the following reasons. The body must turn as soon as the weight shift gets involved to swing the club on the correct backswing plane. Swinging by using leg action from this position would pull the ball left since the body must rotate left in order to use the chest to drive the left arm. This action causes the club to cross the line from out to in and is one variation of the familiar over the top move. When the rotating chest returns the left arm properly the chest will be 15 to 20 degrees open to the target line. You will find more on this later in the chapter on building the full swing.

Next we will deal with how the arms work and the motions we will need to learn and practice to gain control of the elusive club head and club face.

THE WRONG WAY IS THE RIGHT WAY

Inevitably whenever I am giving a lesson to a somewhat accomplished player, who is new to this technique, I hear the words, "Oh, you want me to turn the club the wrong way," to which I reply, "No, I want you to turn the club the right way. You have been turning it the wrong way."

Compared to the commonly taught swing we are turning the club the wrong way but only a tiny bit. When we compare the common swing to Austin's method they are turning the club the wrong way a lot.

By counter rotating the forearms a tiny bit (just enough to keep the face square) to the arc through which it swings, while we cock the wrists under, we are keeping the club head and face under much better control.

The forearm has two bones in it. The one that runs from the bicep to the thumb is called the radius and the one that runs from the elbow to the base of the heel of the hand is called the ulna. It is not important to know their names but we must know how they are used.

As we begin the backswing we turn the left forearm slightly counter-clockwise slowly from the elbow. We do this by turning the ulna of the left arm counter-clockwise out from under the radius as if we had a screwdriver in the left hand and were loosening a screw. In the common swing method the reverse is true.

During the first three feet of club head movement in the backswing, the left forearm rotates the club face closed about 1/8 of a turn. This action cancels the opening of the blade which is caused by the right arm as it folds and rotates to the right as we swing the club around our body. The movements that we learned in the Little Shot are the correct movements of the forearms and wrists through the ball in the full swing just as they are in the chip. In the Full Swing we will be involving the elbows to a fuller degree and as we add the elbow movements we will have to pay close attention to the actions of the forearms as they position the club without lifting the thumbs.

THE ACTIONS OF THE HANDS AND FOREARMS

Notice that although the wrists are fully cocked the shaft is still beneath the hands since the thumbs have not risen. The wrists have cranked the shaft under. Jaacob has choked down on the grip to show that the shaft passes beneath the forearms as the club releases. Try this yourself. Swing the club back and forth while keeping the toe of the club pointing skyward. If the shaft hits your forearms or your arms roll over you have made an error.

Here we have involved the elbow action which has swung the club inside the flight line. The club is now parallel to the shoulders and also to the flight line. Swinging the club head like this is like chipping the ball belt-high off a vertical glass wall between the camera and the player. It is important to note that the club shaft remains horizontal and parallel to the ground as the club head comes around as if sliding on a table. As this action is performed the shaft passes beneath the forearms. Notice that the right elbow has lowered allowing the club head to remain on one plane. The wrists cock 90 degrees without altering the face angle. The club head remains on the top of the shaft and the simple act of straightening the right arm and wrist will create perfect contact.

Here we see what happens when the right arm straightens and the wrists hinge the other way. Again, no shaft roll has occurred and the club head has moved a long way while still remaining square.

The club head has released 90 degrees beyond the center of the arm-shoulder triangle and would have passed through the ball with the face square. Notice that the left elbow has relaxed and lowered, as it must, to allow the full release of the right wrist.

If the left arm is held straight the release cannot be completed. The shaft will not pass beneath the forearms and the shot will be blocked to the right. As stated earlier, the right hand passes between the left hand and the ball. In other words, it goes under the left hand and not over it. Remember, in the photo, this shot is horizontal as if off the wall rather than on the ground.

CHAPTER 15

PLAYING
THE TROMBONE

THE TROMBONING OF THE ARMS

As the pivot rotates the triangle of the the arm-shoulder lever assembly, we shorten the right side of the triangle by "tromboning" the right arm. The reason we give it this special name is that the action duplicates the arm action of a slide trombone player. This action gets the club head as far away as possible from the ball so that we will have more space and time to accelerate it on its way back to the ball. This action is more than the simple bending of the elbow and it accomplishes two objectives.

- By tromboning the right arm, as you see in the photos on page 173, we shorten the back side of the arm-shoulder triangle without raising the club head from the plane. This action greatly simplifies the return arc.

- Since the right arm shortens by tromboning exactly in the opposite direction that it extends in the release and also since it starts tromboning away in the area of the releasing motion, its return by simply doing the opposite movements and returning naturally, will put the extending right arm, unwinding forearms and free swinging wrists in the ideal position to release the power through the impact area.

In the Austin Method we control the backswing by making it the exact reverse of the downswing. The only difference is, the left shoulder blades remain abducted until after impact. Except for that, the downswing sequence is primarily a product of the relaxation of the contracted muscles, thus giving us the club path and club head acceleration we seek without having to consciously control the club.

Let's not forget how the hands swing the club. The cranking hands allow the wrist axles to freely swing the club shaft beneath the forearms as we feel the forearms unwind from the top of the backswing all of the way to the end of the finish. The right hand must pass beneath the left hand, not roll over it.

The above hand action controls the club face through impact and uses the wound up and stretched forearm muscles' natural return to center to help accelerate the club head. By not rolling the forearms and instead letting them unwind we get better control. By relaxing the wrists we do not impede the pendulum. Plus, the muscles that move the hands are stronger in this direction.

HOW TO KILL THE BALL

We are also keeping the club face on one constant plane since, in our arm action, the club is never lifted vertically and raised off plane as it gets on top of the right hand. Instead, our right elbow swings back as does our right upper arm as we trombone the right hand.

This motion allows the right hand and retracting right upper arm bone to swing out and around the right elbow. Its motion swings the left arm directly toward the right shoulder thus allowing the right forearm, as it winds up, to get on top of the right elbow without rising.

This action keeps the club face on plane and much simplifies hitting.

A good mental picture to have is that the swing of your club head will always be in the direction of wherever your shoulders are at any given moment of the swing. The club face will also be square to the ball at all points in the swing. This is not a version of an older method called square to square as the tromboning arm action makes it a motion all its own.

The swinging of the club head from the releasing wrists will be the same action as the tossing of the bag of balls we saw earlier. Most of this toss will be a result of the mass of the club head swinging freely from the wrist axel as the arms are flung out from the body by the inertia of the club head heading for gravity and the centrifugal force caused by the leveraged motion of the pivot.

A good mental picture would be of crank starting an antique car as we pass through impact. (See photo on page 111).

To release totally, think of scooping up sand with the fingernails of your right hand as you hit through. Assuming that your mental picture also had you swinging with your fingers extended straight down and that you have 30 inch long fingernails.

This cranking action allows the club head and club face to travel straight down the flight line during the release, with the clubface coming from slightly de-lofted before impact, to square and with normal loft at impact, to slightly laying back after impact. This is the exact action made by the club that we learned in the Little Shot. When we do this during the Big Shot the ball flies straight and far.

The upper lever assembly, which should be thought of as the shoulder blades, the upper arms and the elbows, will be rotated away from the ball by the backswing pivot and, at the same time, the cocking wrists will be controlled by the counter rotating forearms combined with the tromboning action of the right arm. (See photos next page).

To use the cranked levers correctly we must understand that the wrist joints are not part of it. They are an independent entity and as such will move independently. Their function is threefold.

- In conjunction with the forearms they counter rotate the club face to insure perfect alignment.

- They release the club shaft from behind the arms to in front of the arms by a slow unrolling of the shaft.
  This unrolling motion is *CLOCKWISE*, and is caused by the relaxing of the wound up forearm muscles.

- They allow the bodies power to flow through the club head, into the ball, by not impeding the pendulum of the club.

This unrolling starts from the top of the back swing and ends at the top of the finish. It is caused by a free response to the club head's motion caused by its inertia, combined with gravity and the natural return of the stretched and wound-up forearm muscles. This action is assisted by the extending right arm.

The arms and hands will be brought back to the ball by the leg actions learned in the rope and pole drills. As they are, the left upper arm will remain in its position glued to the left side of the ribcage. If the pivot is performed correctly, the return path of the left arm to impact will be perfect, since the angle formed by the left arm and the club (arm-shaft-angle) does not ever change in the golf swing except after the finish when it doesn't matter anymore.

When the club is swung in the fashion we will be using, the club, arm and shoulders work in a fashion that we can best describe as a cranked lever assembly. Using the arms this way creates a compound action of levers and extracts more force than a simple lever can exert.

In this photo, Jaacob is ready to play some air trombone for you. I hope you like rock and roll music, since that's all he can play on the trombone.

All kidding aside, here is what happens as the right arm begins to trombone. The elbow lowers as the right hand retracts directly toward the right shoulder. This action begins to create the #7 position of the left arm as it also moves the left arm directly toward the right shoulder without raising the hands or the arm. Notice that the right elbow and upper arm move downward toward the right hip. The upper right arm lowers from the shoulder socket. As this happens the wrist keeps the hand vertical.

The three photos on this page show how the right arm must function. The action of the right arm is exactly what a trombone player does. The wrist remains vertical as the elbow goes down. This very important action cannot happen unless the upper right arm bone hinges down from the shoulder socket.

This movement shortens the right arm as it retracts the right hand directly toward the right shoulder.

This is the final movement of the tromboning action. The right upper arm has rotated to the right from within the shoulder socket. This movement takes the left arm across the chest directly toward the right shoulder. As we swing back, it should feel as if the left hand is going to where the right shoulder will be at the end of the shoulder turn.

The finished arm movement is hard to spot to the untrained eye. It will appear to just be a good-looking golf swing to the outside observer.

As the weight shifts and the body turns, the tromboning right arm and counter-rotating left forearm control the motions of the club. Since the right arm is folded on the backswing it is in position to hit and can and will be unfolded with power thus adding impact force. The final movement of the tromboning action is the continued wind-up of the right forearm in the direction of the arrow on the photo below.

In the correct hand position at the top of the backswing, we call the Broken Wrist position, the left wrist is slightly bowed and the right thumb will be on the side of the shaft rather than under the shaft. The palm of the right hand will instead be under the shaft. (See photos).

This photo shows a hand position we call the Broken Wrist position. As you can see, the left wrist is slightly bowed. This is a very strong position for the hands to be in since they can release the club fully without having to turn over through the hit. This bowed-out wrist position is what Ben Hogan sought at impact to remove his hook. Our wrists instead release this angle through impact. This allows the shaft to pass under the forearms, rather than rolling the forearms over, keeping the club face square.

Hitting with the right hand creates serious club head speed. If you were to push a door close to the hinges you would see what I mean. The edge of the door where the knob is would swing quickly but at first it would require much effort. Later in the swing of the door, as it is ready to slam closed, the door would require less push and the speed would be very high.

In this swing method the right arm, due to the tromboning action, unfolds beneath the shaft plane. Since the right arm never goes over the left it can be used completely without the fear of it taking over the golf swing as some teachers of the swing put it.

In this photo, we see the Little Shot hand positions as if we just stood up. The shaft has moved beneath the forearms horizontally 45 degrees rather than on the angled plane. Remember the swing here is not down; it's as if we were chipping the ball off the wall. Since the elbows have not moved, the club head has not swung in closer to the body. The shaft is pointing just inside the left hip.

In this photo, the right elbow has tromboned. The upper arm bone by swinging down from the shoulder socket rather than up as it does in the common swing, has lowered the elbow to just above the hip. Right now you can see that the club face is looking at the wall and a simple reverse of the right-hand and elbow motions would swing the square club face through the ball. Note the clubface has not turned.   (continued following page)

(cont. caption from lower photo preceeding page)

The hands as we swing back, once set, do not move from the wrist-cocked position we have been practicing in our little shot. The tromboning right elbow rotates the shaft paralell to the shoulders. Since the body has not turned the shaft is also paralell to the ground. From this position the right hand takes the left arm directly toward the right shoulder by rotating the right upper arm from within the shoulder socket. As the right arm passes center it totally straightens, the left arm trombones down and the pendulum of the club passes the point of the arm shoulder triangle unimpeded.

This is a mirror image of the lower photo preceeding page. It shows that the left arm has to fold down to get out of the way of the releasing club. If the shot were a soft pitch, without the pivot, you might see the arms released in this position. On a full hard shot the club and arms would reach this position, relative to his body, but from this view you would see his back.

After impact, the tromboning action of the combined hinges of the wrist, elbow and shoulder cause the left arm to not block the direction of the swinging action of the right arm. If the left arm does not trombone we get a block type action that impedes the free swing of the club head.

As we swing down, the action of the weight shift pulls the handle end of the club directly on plane down and around in a very powerful movement. This action is done by the legs coupled with the internal trunk muscles which create the lateral shift of body weight. This powerful acceleration keeps the right arm folded (even though we are trying to straighten it).

At no time in the Austin method are we attempting to pull the club endwise, although the leg drive does cause it to travel endwise for a short time. We are always attempting to make the clubhead go around the shaft radially rather than following it lineally. We are, in effect, trying to make the club as long as possible by swinging the extended club around the swing-circle-center rather than attempting to get the center of club rotation at the wrist joint by pulling an angled club and arm package to the ball and at the last instant opening the angle and swinging the club around a virtually stopped wrist.

The above method of swinging around the wrist works but is not as powerful due to swinging a shorter club. In the Austin method the club still swings freely from the wrist but it is effectively the length of the club plus the distance from the hands to the swing-circle-center. Added to this longer club effect is the fact that the left hand does not stop as the club passes center since it is driven through impact by the power of the shifting body weight and the drive of the legs as they rotate the hips. The left arm is driven through the impact area by the chest which is supporting it and forcing it to keep moving.

As the club head approaches hip high its release will now be assisted by gravity and the right triceps will be able to unfold as the right elbow rises up to the height of the left elbow. The right hand can then release as the forearm muscles allow the right hand to flap in a throwing motion through impact. If the arms relax, the unwinding forearms control the club face as the right arm reverses the trombone movement exactly where it is most needed causing the club head to continue to accelerate at a very high rate as it catches up with the left arm which is being kept moving by the power of the now turning hips. *The club head will be whipped through the ball.*

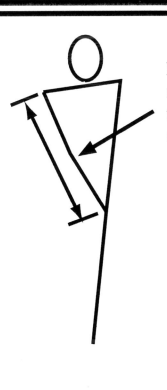

Direction of tromboning arm - elbow retracts down, right arm shortens taking right hand directly toward right shoulder.

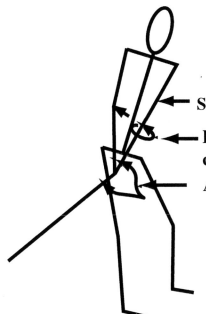

Shift and pivot moves left arm

Left arm counter rotates just enough to keep club square

Arm-Shaft angle remains constant

CHAPTER 16

SPINNING THE MEAT BALLS

At the top of the backswing, after we make the last move of winding up the right forearm, we will have put the hands and the club into the ideal place. The forearm muscles will be in the perfect position to twirl the club head around the maypole of the left arm as the left arm is returned by the downswing weight shift and pivot. This twirling action is shown very clearly in the next photo series. In these photos, the right arm is photographed in a static position in front of the body. During the golf swing the forearm actions you see in the photos would be happening as the forearm was swinging around the body.

The body returns the left arm to the ball with the weight shift and the pivot.

The left arm acts like a maypole as the right arm throws the club head around it. The unwinding forearm muscles return the club face squarely into the back of the ball. The hitting action of the right hand starts at the top of the backswing, and continues all of the way to the finish. The right forearm rotates fully in a complete circle, as you will see in the following picture series.

Since the club face is square half way through the rotation of the forearm and the ball is halfway around the circle of the full swing, the club will automatically be square to the ball and flight line at impact..

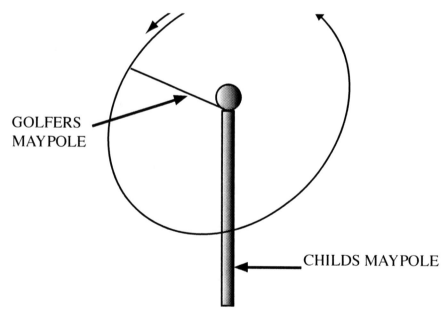

GOLFERS MAYPOLE

CHILDS MAYPOLE

The maypole, when we throw the ball it goes around in a circle. We do the same thing with the club head. The base of the maypole is the left shoulder socket, however our maypole (left arm) is also traveling toward the ball.

This photo series shows the complete movement of the club around the right forearm. The conical action of the club allows the forearm to duplicate what the club does in the full swing. The cocking of the wrist and counter rotation of the forearm are visibly apparent. This series of actions is exactly what the right hand does in the full swing, the motion of the releasing club is circular around the right forearm. The right forearm itself is rotated around by the actions of the pivot.

The un-counter rotation of the right wrist sends the club head rapidly around the outside of the circle as the maypole of the left arm is returned by the pivot. The left arm serves as the maypole until after impact where it is replaced by the right arm which serves as the maypole in the follow through. In this photo series notice that the club makes the full circle.

The above photos show how the unwinding of the foreaems blends into the flapping car crank wrist release. This movement is natural and feels easy.

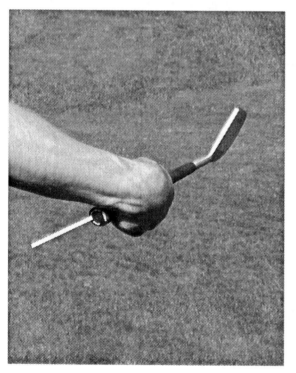

These photos show the continued release and the white line shows how the shaft has passed under the forearms; it has allowed a full hit with the right hand without rolling the blade closed. The final photo, above right, shows the rest of the forearm unwind thus completing the full circle of the swing.

What the right forearm does to start the downswing.

Even though we are looking at the club from the front, the idea I am trying to convey is as if we were looking straight down at the right hand from directly above. Since the right forearm is vertical at the top of the backswing, if the hand was open we could be holding a plate of spaghetti in the same plane that the rotating arrow shows. Notice that the player would be looking at the back of the forearm, the right palm is facing away from the player.

As seen in the little club sequence the counter rotation and re-rotation of the right forearm duplicates the actions the club makes in the full swing. Here I show the motion as a we would twirl a ball on a string. A simple unwinding of the forearm would fling off the meatballs or send the tethered ball rapidly around in a circular motion. This is exactly what the right arm does to start the club head on its journey around the outside of the downswing arc. This action starts the club head away from the direction the maypole (left arm) is traveling and builds much club head speed. It should feel light and does not require much effort to perform. The effort is only for the first 1/4 of the forearm's rotation and then should be felt to freewheel as the right tricep straightens the arm and the right wrist passes the shaft under the left hand in the car crank motion.

HITTING

Make no mistake about it, we are hitting the ball by spinning the meatballs. We will be using the right arm to accelerate the club head right from the top of the swing and this release motion (the unwinding forearms) continues all of the way to the finish. As soon as the feet initiate the weight shift back to the left foot, we spin the meatballs off the plate and twirl the club as seen in the little club photo series. We send the club head away from the body in the opposite direction of the travel of the left arm. This action causes a large arc and puts a large load on the pivot, the weight shifting and the leg drive easily overcome this load, and the club head accellerates hard. The club head gains tremendous speed and the ball takes off as if shot from a cannon.

In the method you are learning, we are able to use our right hand and arm to its full advantage. Since the club head has such a long way to go, the feeling of the whole swing motion will feel to be slow yet the club head will be doing anything but going slow. You wouldn't want your fingers there at impact. We will at no time attempt to delay the hit or anything else for that matter, in our swing we will hit from the top. This is another big difference from common teaching.

Many instructors teach the delay of the uncocking of the wrists. This idea is founded on the principle of the conservation of angular momentum. The way they want you to swing is to revolve the arms and club while making no attempt to swing out based on the theory that the club will snap open at the bottom of the swing and thus speed up the club head. This method works somewhat but the player is not achieving his true potential since the swing of the club head is around the wrists. In effect, the player is hitting with a short lever. When the club head releases close to the ball the angle does open quickly. However, this action also retards the progress of the left hand (visible in high speed photography) since the outward pull of the club almost stops the left arm, the club is then swinging almost entirely from the wrist joints.

In the Austin method, the right arm accelerates the club head around a broad arc and the power of the weight shift, as the hips slide laterally and the right leg drives the pelvis around on top of the posted left leg, maintains the motion of the left arm thus allowing us to swing a much longer lever. This is because we have more leg force to keep the left arm moving and our lever extends all of the way up to the swing-circle-center.

Having said all that about hitting I will also say that all of the hitting effort is done long before we get around to the ball and the only effort we will be using, as the club head freewheels through the impact release arc, will be the continued pivot motion as the right leg drives the right buttock and hip down and around the posted left leg.

In our golf swing you will feel as if the entire swinging action of the golf club happens behind you and the club head never catches up with the chest until the ball is long gone. Instead, we will make contact with the ball off the side of our right hip.

The club head is going so fast through the release area that it's inertia has pulled both arms to the left of the center of Jaacobs chest. If the left arm does not trombone in this area the right arm and club head will be rerouted and the result will be a loss of balance and eventually a very sore left elbow.

Spend enough time at driving ranges and you will see many people with bands around the left forearm near the elbow. Most of them think it's from hitting off a mat or hitting too many balls. However, it's mostly caused by one's own energy hitting themselves by not letting the left arm fold and get out of the way. I am sure this injury has driven many people out of golf. If they learn to play the trombone they may come back.

CHAPTER 17

PUTTING IT TOGETHER

DOMINOES

Because of the way we make the backswing, by doing all of the things in the reverse order of the motions they make in the downswing, we are in effect preparing the body for the downswing exactly as an archer prepares the arrow for the launch. The archer draws the bowstring back and through his actions loads the bow with energy that is also directed exactly in the opposite direction from which the snap of the returning bowstring will send the arrow. If he were to position the end (nock) of the arrow above or below center or pull the bowstring sideways a little from the plane of the bow he would build in an error to the way that the energy is released into the arrow and thus alter the arrows flight.

So it is in the golf swing. The more we can perfect the address position and backswing, as we load the body and stretch the muscles, the more perfectly we will release our stored energy into the ball. In effect, we are setting our bodies up for the release just like lining up a pattern of dominoes. Properly set up, a giant and complex collection of dominoes will fall in perfect order just by knocking over the first one. To this end, we must learn to use the same care in our stance, set up (measuring precisely to the ball) and in controlling the positions of our backswing.

Moving slowly and carefully while being sure to shift before we turn and monitoring the arm and forearm movements as we swing the club back will guarantee us a more precise impact. The downswing is something we can only control by the initial movements of the "spaghetti off the plate move" timed exactly with the movements of the heels that starts the shift of the weight by sliding the hips laterally left. The shift then blends into the turn as the right hip drives down and around and the right foot rotates out and up onto its toe. So set up your dominoes carefully and start your downswing properly and watch the beautiful results as the rest of the dominoes follow their pre-set pattern.

Again it is vitally important to understand all that is in this book in order to make full use of it. Go back and re-read any parts that are still foggy. Why not re-read the whole book? You just might see it a little differently, and in the golf swing a little is a lot. You now have the formula for power and accuracy. Understand it and practice it and you will play your best golf and attain the utmost satisfaction, from this, the ultimate game.

BUILDING THE SWING

We now want to start hitting pitch shots by adding the tromboning actions of the elbows and shoulders, and the wrist and hand moves we have been practicing. (See photos following pages).

During this phase of the learning do not shift your weight. Put your weight on the left heel and keep it there, don't let your weight shift right as it must remain on your left heel throughout the shot. The reason that you want your weight on the left heel is because that is where your weight should be at impact, for every shot, from a putt to a full drive. The only time that you might want your weight slightly more on the right foot than the left at impact, is if you want to intentionally hit a fat shot. A bunker or a flop shot would also be hit this way. With these shots we intentionally hit behind the ball and slide the club head under the ball on the bounce of the sand wedge.

Start learning this shot with very short pitches. These shots should not exceed 30 yards in length. This is the way we will hit our pitch shots, without a weight shift, and using as few levers as possible. As you do this, on the early short pitches, do not turn the chest. You will see, as the arms begin to trombone, that the club head no longer swings straight back and up. It will now make an inward arc. Be sure to use the same, car crank, hand feel that you have developed while doing your little shots. The conical action still happens and its look will disappear but its feel must remain the same.

Once you have this little pitch working well, shift the weight as you go back and begin turning your shoulders and thus hit larger and larger shots until you are hitting full shots.

The motion will be a little stiff and tight feeling at first but with practice you will soon feel relaxed. If you hit ten good sand wedge shots in a row move up two clubs to the nine iron . If you do not hit a good solid shot within three swings put the club back and go back to your sand wedge. If you hit three bad sand wedges go all the way back to the little shot and gradually add parts until you have the feel again. Again, move up two clubs after three good shots, never hit more than three bad shots without going back two clubs.

This is the beginning of the pitch shot, the left pinky knuckle has turned under, the slight counter rotation of the shaft has occurred. The club head has swung slightly inside the line due to the beginning of the tromboning right elbow action. Notice that the weight is still on the left foot. From here the right elbow will trombone only until the shaft is parallel to the shoulders. Correctly done, we attain the position seen in the photo on the facing page. To hit shots farther than this action allows we turn the shoulders. As the hands pass the right leg the weight begins to shift.

This photo shows the tromboning arm movement added to the wrist cock and counter rotation. Notice that the shoulders have turned the same amount as the hips, the body tilt and turn is being done with the knees. The right knee is beginning to straighten and the left knee is beginning to flex out toward the flight line. From this position pitch the ball with your right hand passing under the left through impact. Turn the body smoothly and easily at the same speed you rotate the chest. Start the downswing with your right knee and pick up your right heel to allow the body to rotate. After the pitches feel good and solid, simply rotate the shoulders farther, a little at a time, until you are hitting full shots. You should feel as if you are not swinging the club with your arms at all, but rather, leaving it where it was at the top of the swing. Simply pivoting and rotating the chest through the shot will swing the chest around the spine and return the upper lever assembly for perfectly executed golf shots.

As long as the shots are good, continue going up two clubs at a time. This way we are building confidence and we are training ourselves with, and for, success. Soon all the clubs will feel good. After all, it's the same swing, right?

The hands and forearms can only do their jobs if the actions of the tromboning elbows are done correctly. The right hand must trombone in directly toward the right shoulder. If it does not, the left arm will be forced to a different position and we will be unable to get the right hand correctly behind the club shaft with the right forearm wound up for the strike. The correct tromboning will also keep the arms from rising from the shoulder sockets and it will allow the right upper arm bone to rotate 45 degrees to the right without raising the elbow, thus keeping the club head on the original plane.

As the club is swung back, the hands should feel as if they are rolling the shaft from under the left forearm to beneath the right forearm. The action of counter-rotating the shaft will make the club head rise relative to the hands without causing the arms or thumbs to rise. The club will then move in a conical manner. Since we want a broad arc through the ball on the through swing with the club face releasing in an up-kick fashion, we must remember to start the club face away in the backswing in a manner that feels like the heel of the club is leading the toe. This slight closing of the club face, together with the actions of the pivot and the tromboning right arm, will swing the club head on the perfect arc. It will swing inside and back on the perfect plane every time with the club face always square.

The feeling we will get on the downswing is that the hands do not work from wall to wall, as you have felt in your roller swing. Instead they will work from ceiling to floor and back to the ceiling. The release is much like crank starting an antique automobile or using a crank-type scissor jack. As we pass the club beneath the forearms we must turn the knuckles of the left hand toward the target and up. Your left palm must be felt to face the ground after impact and the left thumb will get behind, and then under, the shaft. This action will allow the releasing right hand to go under the left hand. Just as the right hand goes under the left when cranking up a jack. This is much harder to write about than it is to do. The few simple moves we have been practicing, when combined, will fit each other like jigsaw pieces. They are perfectly designed to work together and they will function like a well oiled machine when done correctly.

The largest part of this swinging method is the pivot. The only separate motion is the swinging and release of the club head and the club face. That action is perfectly controlled by the return action of the unwinding forearms and free releasing wrists. A big key to playing well is the ability to relax and trust the winding up that we have done as we swung back. As we come down, by allowing the stretched muscles to relax, our bodies will produce the movements we need to create the optimum ball flight. It is this full and total trust that will determine just how good we become.

Our arms will be slung into the ball by the correct actions of the shifting weight and the use of the internal torso muscles combined with the power released by the driving legs as they laterally slide and rotate the hips. This supplies immense energy into the club head as centrifugal force and gravity combine causing the club to reach tremendous speed as it catches up to and passes the left arm through the hitting area. The release of this stored energy will guarantee the return of the club to its in line with the left arm position as long as it swings pendulum like from the relaxing wrists. The club head will gain additional propulsion by the straightening of the right arm coupled with the relaxing left arm as it mirrors the right arms actions going back by folding and tromboning from the wrist and elbow. This action will allow the free swinging pendulum (the club) to swing through a 180 degree arc without closing the club face thus allowing us to return to the at address setting of the club face and delivering the expected ball flight.

The club head will be traveling at a very high rate of speed. As the left arm approaches the ball, propelled by the weight shift and the hip turn, it must be allowed to swing freely from the left wrist and get ahead of the left arm after impact thereby guaranteeing club head acceleration through the ball. The speeding and free-swinging club head will deliver a mighty blow to the ball. You will probably be amazed at the amount of distance that you gain the first time you let the club head go through the ball like this; read on pilgrim and more shall be revealed.

The right hand must pass between the left hand and the ball. The shaft (if we let it) will be slowly rolling to the right as the release occurs, in effect, working from closed to square to open this action causes the club face to remain square throughout the entire swing, especially as it passes through impact and launches the ball up.

Once the weight shift and chest turn have been completed and the shoulder blades have reached the end of their travel, the bow string is fully stretched.

The machine of the body has reached the limit of the movement of the parts and has done so without moving the swing-circle-center. Having achieved this wound-up position our job, now, is to keep the body from unwinding. We do this by holding the chest and shoulder blades in this condition. With the upper body held back, we will use the leg action, and weight shift, to reverse the tilt of the spine. As the right knee and ankle drive the pelvis down and around, the rotating chest will drive the left arm into the ball. This causes us to hit the ball off the side of our right hip rather than in the unwound condition of hitting in front of our bellies.

It is the maintenance of this tension that causes the power of the weight shift and legs to do the work rather than the unwinding of the back muscles, which will not produce as much power and, sooner or later, will cause us back pain or worse.

The above actions are accompanied by the swinging of the club with the right arm as we put back into the downswing the release of the swinging pendulum of the club.

If the right hand does not swing between the left hand and the ball the only alternative is for the right arm to roll over the left (oops, we're back to the roller swing) which will also accelerate the club head. This action will then require perfect timing to have the club face (which is now revolving around the shaft) square up at impact as the right hand passes over the left hand at the ball.

- In our swing we will not roll our arms thus eliminating any chance of the unexpected and unwanted hook.

This is a posed photo to show the hand release. Here, it is clear that the hands do not roll over, the right hand is in the act of passing between the left hand and the ball. The left arm is tromboning as can be seen by the beginning of the lowering of the left elbow (arrow). The left wrist is releasing under the wrist axel. If this were an actual hit the club head would be a blur due to its incredible speed. Notice also the face angle of the club - it is facing down the line and laid back. No chance of a hook here.

Your ball should fly quite a bit higher on standard shots. Don't worry, to control your trajectory just move the ball back in your stance before you take your grip. Moving the ball back de-lofts the club so keep the face pointing where you want the ball to go. This will cause the club head to hood as the shaft leans toward the target. You can actually put the ball to the right of your right foot and it will fly very low. With the ball that far back the club is coming down very steeply so you will take a very deep divot. At some point the swing will be so steep that you cannot swing through the shot since the divot will be too deep. With practice you will be able to hit your seven iron under a card table at 100 yards.

All we have to do to hit solid shots is make sure to control the plane with our weight shift and control the club face with the counter rotation of the forearms. By controlling the plane with the weight shift and turn we can virtually eliminate the over-the-top move which causes both pulled shots that go to the left if the release of the club head happens or a block to the right if it does not.

The arms will contribute their part by sending the club head around the outside of its release arc caused by the unwinding of the forearms which in turn frees up the right arm and causes the correct right elbow position, the straightening right arm will assist in increasing the club head's speed. As you have seen in the photos this combination of movements will move the maximum amount of the body's weight through the shot (from behind the ball to in front of the ball). When we execute this movement properly the swing-circle-center will remain anchored in its original position thus stabilizing the head and to the eyes (also stable due to lack of head movement) the ball will appear to be very still and easy to hit accurately.

Any movement of the head and eyes will cause the ball to appear to be moving. It is much easier for a rifle shooter to hit a target while motionless, than upon a galloping horse. If your head moves so do your eyes and accuracy is compromised, some players with super hand and eye coordination can still hit solid shots but they are working harder than necessary.

The free wrist release under the wrist axel will control the club face while allowing it to swing through the ball unimpeded by muscular control, which slows it down.

Hopefully, the train is completely out of the fog and your inner vision of what you must do to hit the ball with power and accuracy is clear. It is this correct picture in our minds eye that will direct our body's motions exactly as a computer program moves a computer-controlled machine.

The ability to create perfect shots is ultimately a product of the mind's ability to pre-conceive and visualize not only the flight of the ball but the club face ball alignments and the motions the body must do in order to produce that shot.

Remembering the picture in our minds eye is what controls the motion, as Mike has stated so eloquently "Golf is mental imagery."

HOW TO KILL THE BALL

As you will learn later, this throwing action is exactly what we are doing. We are throwing the club head through the ball and controlling the club face with the natural unwind of the forearms. The weighted club head releases the free swinging hands. The plane and the path have been controlled by the pivot, thus the arc of the club heads travel has been determined by the stationary head.

In the photo on page 199, the white lines show that the club head is fully released (past the point of the arm shoulder triangle).The club head is already beginning to come back in over the left shoulder while the hands are still going out toward the target. As you can see, he is still looking at where the ball was. At this point, the rotating chest will pull his head up and the ball will appear in the center of his vision about 25 yards out, leaving in a big hurry. The right wrist has fully released so the left wrist, that cannot be seen in the photo, must be released also. The shaft has passed under the arms. The pendulum has swung freely and whipped through the ball. I wouldn't want my fingers in between the club and ball. Jaacob now has a consistent 141-mph club head speed and is gaining more each day.

PUTTING IT ALL TOGETHER

I have found that if I get a feel for all of the parts of the swing working early in my practice session or pre-game warm up, the whole session or round requires less conscious control and the whole swing works much better. The body can not make the golf swing well if the conscious mind is trying to control it. We must simplify our thoughts. To play golf well we must rely on what a good swing feels like. Since feels are in the realm of the sub-conscious, we must learn to trust the body to perform the motions we have learned and practiced.

When you start your practice session, begin without a ball and work your wrists and forearms as you swing your sand wedge in the feel of the little shot. Watch the club head as it goes back and make sure it goes straight back and up as you turn your left pinky knuckle under. Now hit a few chips and make sure it feels right. Next make a practice swing and add the tromboning of the elbows, again without a ball and without a weight shift, (weight totally on left heel and no chest turn) and make swings that would produce a 20 yard pitch. Swing easily and feel the elbows work. Also, monitor the feel of the hands as the club swings freely under them in the car crank manner. Now lets hit the shot and see what we get. If its good, add a little more arm and elbow action while still not shifting or turning. As you approach the limit of how far you can hit the ball with just these actions, add some chest wind up while still not shifting the weight. To keep from shifting the weight stay on the left heel. Once we turn the chest our shots must be powered by the hips. So even though you did not shift to the right foot, as you swing down keep the chest turned back and lead the motion with the lifting of the right heel and a turning of the hips. Make sure the hit occurs alongside of the right hip. When it feels right, go ahead and hit a few of these. If you are hitting the above shot well we simply add the weight shift as we do the other actions. Make sure you feel the rope drill in a few swings with no ball, and now swing a few more times monitoring the feels of the rope drill. As you feel the whole action together be sure you are shortening the right side of the body on the down swing by pulling the right side of the rib cage close to the top of the hip. You are ready to hit the shot now so let it fly. If the shot went well, hit several more and then move up through the bag making the same motion for all clubs. Hit shots with the balls you have left without thoughts as to how to do it. Focus instead, on how it feels to hit it good.

You are now ready to play.

CHAPTER 18

PHOTO SERIES

This starts a photo series of the important parts of Mike Dunaway's incredibly powerful and extremely accurate swing.

Mike is in his set-up position, perfectly measured to the ball. The white lines show that his feet and knees are paralell to the direction of ball flight. Notice that his chest is pointed slightly left of the flight line as are his hips, all powerful swingers set up this way, since the chest will be well around almost facing the target at impact.

In this photo the open shoulders and hips are more evident. This is caused by the slight turn of the pelvis left, as he flexed his right knee, to lower his right hand, so that he could take his grip.

Here we see the start of the take-away. The weight has shifted to the right heel, the right elbow is beginning to trombone, and the slight counter rotation that keeps the club face looking at the ball can be seen.

This is not an actual shot, this is Mike's mental image of where he want's his arms and club to be at this point in the follow through. When the swing is happening at top speed he will be in a slightly different position due to the outward pull of the club head. It is good to have an image in the back of your mind of the free release of the arms.

At the top of the backswing it is interesting to note that the club face is looking skyward. This position is called closed in the roller swing, but square in the Austin swing. His body is well coiled up and all he has to do to pound the ball straight and far is, spin the meatballs, relax his arms and pivot rapidly. His perfectly measured stance, combined with his execution of the pivot has kept his swing-circle-center stable. By swinging his arms both back and down, with the pivot and turn of the shoulders, he has created the perfect swing plane and path. The white line shows that the hands remain below the shoulders. The twirl of the club head provides the speed.

This photo says it all, notice that the left leg is straight and the right leg is driving the hips both laterally and around. The chest is 45 or more degrees open to the line of flight allowing plenty of room for the club head and arms to extend. Notice that the right elbow and right wrist are straightening but are still not fully extended. These things show that all of the power of the swing is being released right where it will do the most good.
At impact! You just can't do it any better than this folks. Due to the Austin release he has no fear of hooking the ball.

Due to the speed and power of Mike's swing, this photo was taken during a very easy swing so the camera could catch the position without it being a blur. Notice that the club face is looking down even though the right hand went under the left. This shows that the club face remained square throughout the entire swing. Remember, it was looking skyward at the top of the backswing. If this were a full power shot he would have driven the pelvis around with the right leg and the right heel would be directly above the toe of the right foot.

Dan Shauger

Jaacob Bowden

Mike Austin

Mike Dunaway

FOR FURTHER INSTRUCTION, DVD'S,VIDEOS
AND PRODUCTS DESIGNED TO IMPROVE YOUR
GAME CHECK OUR WEB SITE
www.aperfectswing.com
OR SEND FOR OUR BROCHURE
2 DOWN PRESS INC.
1801 EAST TROPICANA SUITE 9
LAS VEGAS NEVADA 89119-6559

Printed in the United States
19822LVS00001B/13-36